SEARCHING for
SUNSHINE

THE QUIET SECRET TO LASTING HAPPINESS

By Michael J. Eaker

PIERIAN SPRING
PUBLISHING

www.searchingforsunshinebook.com
ISBN: 979-8-9998471-4-0

Printed and bound in the United States by
Ingram Spark

For my amazing wife, Aline, and our incredible son,
Freddie — thank you both for making sunshine so easy to find!

CONTENTS

INTRODUCTION
THE ENDLESS CHASE

In nearly every corner of modern life, the message is the same: more is better. We are told we need more money, more success, more possessions, more followers, more square footage — more everything. From the billboards lining our highways to the ads glowing on our phones, the story is relentless: happiness is always one purchase, one promotion, one upgrade away.

It is a story that has shaped entire generations. We measure our worth by what we own, how much we produce, and how busy we appear. We celebrate exhaustion as ambition, clutter as abundance, and endless striving as progress. And yet, for all of this "more," people are often unhappier than ever. Anxiety is epidemic. Stress-related illnesses are climbing. Families spend less time together. Even when we do get the thing we wanted so badly, the glow fades quickly, replaced by the itch for the next acquisition.

Psychologists call this hedonic adaptation — our tendency to return to a baseline of contentment no matter what we gain. The promotion, the new car, the dream vacation spark a rush of satisfaction, and then our brains normalize them. What once thrilled us becomes the new normal. With adaptation comes restlessness, and the cycle repeats: want, obtain, adjust, want again.

This adaptation once helped our ancestors survive. When food was scarce or winters harsh, being able to adjust quickly to improvements meant we kept striving, kept seeking. But in a consumer culture, the same instinct is weaponized. What once ensured survival now fuels shopping.

It's a cycle as old as advertising itself: create

desire, sell the solution, repeat. The result is a society that never feels full, only hungry.

I once believed in this cycle myself. Maybe you did, too. I thought happiness lived just beyond the next raise, the next gadget, the next vacation. And the moments of satisfaction were real — but they were fleeting. When they disappeared, I was left chasing the next fix. I was searching for sunshine in the wrong places.

The truth is, sunshine has been here all along. It lives in the overlooked corners of our daily lives: the quiet cup of coffee before the world wakes up, the laughter of a friend on the phone, the feel of fresh air on your face during a walk. It shows up when we notice what is already present rather than obsess over what is missing.

This book is about reclaiming that sunshine. It's about learning to step off the treadmill of "more" and to recognize when enough is enough. It's about finding joy not by adding to our lives, but by subtracting what weighs us down — the excess clutter, the endless striving, the constant comparison.

We'll look at how the corporate world feeds our appetite for excess, how advertising manipulates our sense of lack, and how consumer culture profits from our discontent. But more importantly, we'll explore what it means to live with less yet feel richer. We'll talk about gratitude, simplicity, and the courage it takes to say: this is enough.

If you've ever felt exhausted by the chase, overwhelmed by the noise, or quietly suspicious that life was meant to be lighter than this, you're not alone. This book is not about guilt or deprivation. It is about freedom — rediscovering the sunshine that has always been within reach. The question is simple: are you ready to look for it?

THE COST OF CHASING

I didn't come to this realization overnight. For years, I bought into the idea that happiness was just around the corner. A new car would make me feel successful. A bigger house would make me feel secure. The latest phone would make me feel connected. And for a moment, each of those things worked. There was always that brief high, that flicker of satisfaction. But soon enough, the shine dulled, and I was left staring at the same emptiness I thought I had solved.

What I was really doing was renting happiness. I was paying for temporary relief from discontent and mistaking it for joy. The payments were constant: new clothes for a lift in confidence, dinners out for the illusion of luxury, subscriptions I barely used but kept anyway — "just in case." None of it delivered what it promised for long. I wasn't investing in joy; I was leasing distractions.

And I wasn't alone. Maybe you've noticed this pattern in your own life. You fill a shopping cart on impulse, only to feel guilty the moment the bags are unpacked. You hit a professional milestone and wonder why it doesn't feel as good as you thought it would. You stand in a cluttered room and realize the weight of your belongings is heavier than the satisfaction they were supposed to bring.

It's not our fault we feel this way. We've been conditioned to. From childhood, we are immersed in a culture that whispers — and often shouts — that who we are is not enough, that what we have is not enough. The answer, we are told, is always to add more. And yet the more we add, the less we feel.

This conditioning is not random. It is engineered. Advertising has grown into one of the most powerful forces in human history, shaping not only what we buy but how we see ourselves. Corporations pour billions into convincing us that contentment is dangerous, that satisfaction is laziness, that happiness must be pursued through consumption. Because a grateful person who loves their old car, who enjoys their modest home, who doesn't need the latest phone — that person doesn't generate growth. For companies, contentment is a liability.

And so they sell us discontent wrapped in aspiration. Commercials show families laughing in gleaming kitchens, cars gliding down empty highways at sunset, couples sipping champagne in spotless living rooms. The message is everywhere and always the same: want this joy? Buy this product.

We grow up equating a full shopping cart with a full life. The "American Dream" drifts from freedom and opportunity toward accumulation and status. We measure ourselves against neighbors, coworkers, and strangers on social media. If they have more, we feel less. Psychologists call this social comparison theory — the instinct to measure ourselves against others. Left unchecked, it leaves us perpetually dissatisfied, because there will always be someone who seems to be ahead.

And so the chase continues. Buy more, achieve more, prove more. Yet the happiness these promises offer is fragile. The moment the glow fades, we are back where we started, searching again.

THE NOISE OF "MORE"

The workplace reinforces this cycle in subtle but powerful ways. Success is defined by constant motion — climbing higher, earning more, proving ourselves without pause. Promotions and raises are celebrated not only for the improvements they bring, but because they symbolize worth. They become proof that we are valuable, not just to the company but in life itself. The problem is, no matter how high we climb, the ladder never ends. There's always a next rung, a new benchmark, a fresh reason to feel not-enough.

Social media takes this dynamic and magnifies it. Every scroll is a highlight reel — vacations on turquoise beaches, remodels that gleam with fresh paint and marble countertops, perfectly coordinated family photos in holiday sweaters. We don't see the arguments, the debt, the late nights at work, or the loneliness just outside the frame. We see only the curated peak, and we measure our lives against it. If happiness is a race, we always seem to be lagging behind.

Psychologists warn that this constant exposure to comparison erodes mental health. Studies show that people who spend more time on social platforms are more likely to report feelings of anxiety, envy, and low self-esteem. It's not simply because others have "more," but because their version of "more" is designed to appear flawless. We compare our behind-the-scenes to everyone else's highlight reel — a contest no one can win.

This is why the story of "more" is so powerful. It isn't just an advertising campaign; it is a cultural script. It's reinforced at work, online, in our neighborhoods, even at family gatherings. We celebrate busyness as though exhaustion were a medal of honor. We treat clutter as abundance, as if the fullness of our closets were proof of a full life. We measure progress not by how deeply we experience our days but by how much we can stack onto them.

And yet, beneath the noise, many of us feel the same quiet suspicion: this can't be all there is. Life was meant to be lighter than this.

That hunch isn't naïve; it's attention finally slipping past the noise. It is a crack in the facade, a whisper of clarity beneath the roar of consumer culture. It's the sense that maybe — just maybe — happiness is not out there, waiting at the next rung of the ladder, the next purchase, the next season. Maybe happiness is closer, quieter, and far less complicated than we've been led to believe.

The truth is, these definitions of happiness — the ones handed down by corporations, advertisers, and algorithms — are borrowed, not chosen. They're scripts designed to keep us restless. But scripts can be rewritten. And the first act of freedom is recognizing that what we've been taught about happiness might not be true.

This book is about reclaiming that authorship. It's about stepping out of the story of "more" and beginning to ask better questions: What actually brings me joy? What does "enough" look like for me? Where do I already feel light, grateful, or alive?

The act of asking these questions is not small. In a culture that thrives on our dissatisfaction, simply pausing to consider them is radical. It's the beginning of a new path — one that leads away from the noise of "more" and toward a quieter, more grounded form of happiness.

WHEN ENOUGH FELT CLEAR

It wasn't just studies and headlines that made the pattern visible; everyday moments began to do it for me.

One of the moments that made me begin questioning all of this happened on an ordinary Saturday morning. I was standing in a big-box store, fluorescent lights buzzing overhead, my cart filled with things I didn't really need but had somehow convinced myself I did: paper towels in bulk, a new set of mugs even though I already had plenty at home, a gadget that promised to "save time" but would almost certainly end up shoved in a drawer.

As I pushed the cart down another aisle, I caught sight of a young family. Their little boy was laughing, spinning in circles with a toy in his hands, while his parents smiled and lingered with him. They weren't rushing. They weren't distracted. Their happiness in that moment had nothing to do with what sat on the shelves. I, on the other hand, was surrounded by the same products but felt heavy. The contrast was stark: they were light, I was weighed down.

That moment stayed with me because it revealed something simple but profound — joy isn't sold in stores. It isn't tucked into the "seasonal specials" or bundled into a two-for-one promotion. It lives in presence, in connection, in laughter. That family was living proof of it.

After that, I began to notice how often I equated buying with living. If I had a free evening, I would browse online shops instead of picking up the phone to call a friend. If I felt restless, I would scroll through ads, convincing myself that a new purchase would reset everything. Slowly, I realized this wasn't freedom at all. It was a trap — one that millions of us step into every day without noticing.

We live in a culture of excess, and yet we are starved for meaning. We accumulate, but rarely appreciate. We chase, but rarely arrive. The result is cluttered homes, strained bank accounts, and restless minds. It's no wonder anxiety and depression are on the rise. Our lives are overflowing with things but often feel empty of joy.

Social scientists call this the paradox of choice. The more options we have, the harder it becomes to feel satisfied with any of them. We stand in front of a wall of breakfast cereals or scroll through endless streaming shows and somehow feel more anxious than grateful. Abundance, it turns out, can become a burden.

And yet, clarity begins to emerge the moment we step back. When we pause long enough to ask what truly matters, we see that much of what clutters our lives is simply noise. What remains — the connections, the presence, the gratitude — is what has always sustained us.

This book is not about austerity or deprivation. It's not about rejecting comfort or ambition. It's about clarity — drawing a line between what adds depth to our lives and what merely adds weight. It's about choosing enough — clearly, honestly, unapologetically.

THE PULL OF COMPARISON

Just as advertising sets the stage for discontent, comparison is the hook that keeps us caught. From the earliest days of childhood, we learn to measure ourselves against others: Who runs faster? Who earns better grades? Who gets picked first for the team? As adults, the markers change, but the habit remains. Who drives the nicer car? Who gets promoted more quickly? Who seems to live in the bigger house or take the better vacations?

Psychologists call this social comparison theory, and it has profound effects on our well-being. Research shows that we rarely compare downward — toward those with less — and when we do, the relief is temporary. Instead, we compare upward, toward those who appear to have more. The trouble is, there will always be someone ahead. No matter what we achieve, someone else will seem to outpace us. Comparison ensures that happiness, if tied to being "better," will always be unstable.

Social media amplifies this tendency until it feels relentless. What once required a glance at a neighbor's driveway or a colleague's résumé now streams into our pockets 24/7. We scroll through curated feeds of vacations, remodels, promotions, and celebrations. Each image is polished, filtered, carefully chosen to showcase the brightest moments of someone else's life. We don't see the stress, the debt, the arguments behind the camera. We see only the highlight reel, and we measure our ordinary against it. No wonder it feels like we're falling behind.

Studies confirm what most of us intuitively know: heavy social media use correlates with higher rates of anxiety and depression, particularly when it involves constant comparison. The more time we spend immersed in other people's highlight reels, the more dissatisfied we become with our own unedited lives.

And yet, it's not just social media. The corporate world thrives on this same dynamic. Workplaces reward competition, often subtly encouraging us to measure ourselves against colleagues rather than collaborate with them. Success is framed as ascent — metrics forever inching higher. Climb one, and there is always another. Promotions and raises are celebrated, but the celebration quickly fades, leaving us hungry for the next step.

The danger here is subtle but corrosive. We begin to equate happiness with progress — not in the sense of personal growth or learning, but in the sense of never standing still. Rest becomes guilt. Stillness becomes laziness. Enough becomes unthinkable.

And so the cycle deepens: advertising whispers that we need more; comparison convinces us that we are behind; workplaces reinforce the idea that standing still equals failure. Together, these forces keep us moving endlessly forward — not toward fulfillment, but toward exhaustion.

But here's the truth worth pausing for: these definitions of happiness are not natural. They are borrowed. They're fed to us by industries that profit when we feel inadequate. When we begin to see this clearly, something shifts. We stop asking, "What should make me happy?" and start asking, "What actually does?" That's where the real journey begins.

AN INVITATION TO ENOUGH

This book is not about guilt. It is not about deprivation. It is about freedom. For too long, many of us have allowed corporations, advertisements, and cultural pressures to dictate what should make us happy. They have told us that happiness is found in the promotion, the bigger house, the sleeker phone, the curated image. But when we look honestly, most of those prescriptions leave us restless.

Reclaiming happiness begins with reclaiming

authorship. It is the decision to step out of the script written for us and to ask, with honesty: What truly matters to me? For some, the answer may be fewer possessions but richer experiences. For others, it may be choosing time over money, or presence over productivity. There is no single formula. The point is not to mimic someone else's minimalist journey or chase another person's definition of joy. The point is that the answer belongs to you.

This act of reclaiming is not always easy. Our culture does not celebrate "enough." It celebrates "more." Which means that choosing differently may invite resistance — from coworkers who measure worth in promotions, from friends who equate fun with consumption, even from parts of yourself conditioned to want endlessly. But each time you choose fulfillment over fleeting pleasure, presence over accumulation, you are stepping out of that cycle. You are writing a different story.

And here's the irony: once you stop chasing "more," you begin to see more. Sunshine appears in places you once overlooked. You measure your life not by how much you can add, but by how deeply you can live. Joy shifts from being a prize to win into a practice of attention.

This book is structured as an exploration of that

practice. Across twelve chapters, we will question the myths we've been sold about happiness. Examine how corporations and advertising keep us chasing. Uncover the hidden costs of excess — financial, emotional, and spiritual. Notice what truly matters and define our own version of "enough." Practice gratitude, presence, and simplicity that ground us. Let go of clutter, comparison, and the constant striving for more.

These chapters are not rules to follow. They are guideposts, questions, and reflections meant to help you pause, notice, and choose. Think of them as markers along a trail. Some may resonate immediately; others may take longer. That is as it should be. This is not a program to complete; it is a perspective to embrace.

At the heart of it all is a simple truth: joy doesn't come from addition; it comes from attention — from noticing what is already enough.

CHAPTER ONE

REDEFINING HAPPINESS

When most of us think about happiness, we imagine it as a destination — the point at which we finally arrive after working hard, buying enough, achieving enough, and proving enough. In this version of the story, happiness always lives in the future. I'll be happy when... When the promotion comes. When the house is bigger. When the debts are paid. When the car is new. When vacation finally arrives.

But this definition of happiness is slippery. It moves just out of reach. The moment we achieve one milestone, another appears, dangling the same promise. And so we live in a cycle of postponement — happiness deferred, always waiting for tomorrow.

I remember getting a raise at work I had longed for. I thought it would change everything. For months I imagined the relief, the security, the sense of accomplishment it would bring. And for a few weeks, it did. But soon, the bills rose to match the new income. The glow faded, replaced by the quiet suggestion that I should aim for the next raise, the next step. The satisfaction I expected to last slipped through my fingers, leaving me chasing again.

Psychologists have a name for this cycle: the hedonic treadmill. Human beings have a striking ability to adapt. We quickly return to a baseline level of happiness no matter what positive changes occur. The new car becomes ordinary. The promotion becomes another line on the résumé. The house becomes the backdrop to daily life. What once felt extraordinary becomes the new normal, and suddenly we need something else to feel the same rush. In this way, happiness defined by possessions and achievements is like chasing the horizon: no matter how fast you run, you never arrive.

But what if happiness is not a destination at all? What if it has less to do with arriving and more to do with noticing?

When I think back on the happiest moments of my life, they rarely look like the glossy images sold to us. They weren't expensive. They weren't even planned. They were mornings lingering over coffee with a loved one. Walks where the air smelled like rain and the world felt new. Conversations with friends that wandered late into the night. None of these moments required more money, more possessions, or more achievement. They required presence.

That's the first step toward redefining happiness: recognizing that it is not "out there" waiting to be earned or bought. It is already here, available in the overlooked corners of everyday life. Happiness doesn't demand more; it asks us to notice what is already enough.

From the moment we are old enough to watch television, happiness is defined for us. Bright commercials show smiling families in gleaming kitchens, cars gliding down empty highways at sunset, and people laughing as they unbox the newest gadget. The message is everywhere and always the same: if you want this kind of joy, you must buy this product.

Over time, this programming becomes invisible. We grow up equating a full shopping cart with a full life. We are taught that the people who "have it all" are the ones who matter most, that status is measured in things, and that joy can be ordered, shipped, and delivered to our doorstep. Corporations spend billions ensuring that this story feels not only persuasive but natural — as though wanting more is simply part of being human.

But the truth is, this cycle benefits the system far more than it benefits us. A content person is a poor consumer. Someone who feels gratitude for what they already own does not fuel endless growth. From a corporate perspective, sufficiency is a problem. And so we are sold discontent in the language of aspiration.

The workplace reinforces the same message in subtler ways. Success is defined by constant motion — climbing higher, earning more, proving ourselves without rest. Promotions and raises are celebrated not only for the improvements they bring, but because they signal our worth. Yet no matter how high we climb, the ladder never ends. We are conditioned to equate happiness with progress, not in the sense of personal growth or learning, but in the sense of never standing still.

Social media has amplified this cycle into something relentless. Every scroll offers a curated glimpse into other people's highlight reels: vacations on turquoise beaches, sparkling kitchens, smiling families in matching outfits. We don't see the bills, the arguments, or the quiet loneliness that sit outside the frame. What we see convinces us that our lives are smaller, duller, and less worthy by comparison. Psychologists call this social comparison theory — the instinct to measure ourselves against others. Left unchecked, it leaves us perpetually dissatisfied, because there will always be someone who seems to be ahead.

And so the chase continues. Buy more, achieve more, prove more. Yet the happiness these promises offer is fragile. The moment the glow fades, we are back where we started, searching again.

But these definitions of happiness — the ones handed down by corporations, advertisers, and algorithms — are borrowed, not chosen. They do not arise from our deepest values but from a marketplace designed to keep us restless.

Redefining happiness begins when we notice this and ask a different question: What actually brings me joy?

This shift is not easy. It requires unlearning decades of programming. It requires noticing when the urge to buy or achieve is actually a symptom of restlessness rather than a genuine need. It requires the courage to step off the path everyone else seems to be racing down and admit that we are choosing differently.

And yet, once we begin, the act itself feels like liberation. To say, I am happy with this. I am happy now, is one of the most radical statements we can make in a culture that insists we should always want more.

It helps to recognize that not all forms of happiness are the same. Broadly speaking, there are two kinds: fleeting pleasure and lasting fulfillment. Both have value, but they function differently, and the trouble begins when we confuse one for the other.

Fleeting pleasure is easy to spot. It's the thrill of unboxing something new, the buzz of likes on a social media post, the first sip of an expensive drink. These moments are real and enjoyable. They can brighten our days. But they are also temporary by design. They fade quickly, and once they do, they leave us craving the next fix. This is why the excitement of a new gadget doesn't last, or why the joy of a promotion soon turns into pressure for the next one. Fleeting pleasures are like sugar: sweet, but unsustainable as the foundation of a diet.

Fulfillment, on the other hand, is quieter. It doesn't always spike our emotions in the same way. Sometimes it sneaks up on us in moments of stillness. It's the sense of belonging that comes when we share a meal with people we love. It's the peace that settles over us after finishing a good book, or watching the sun sink slowly below the horizon. It's the pride that comes from meaningful work, not because of the paycheck, but because it aligns with our values. Unlike fleeting pleasure, fulfillment lingers. It grows deeper the more attention we give it.

Research backs this up. Psychologists Edward Deci and Richard Ryan, in their Self-Determination Theory, show that lasting well-being is tied to three universal needs: autonomy (the sense of choice), competence (the sense of growth), and relatedness (the sense of belonging). Fulfillment usually touches these needs. Fleeting pleasure rarely does.

Unfortunately, much of our modern world is designed to maximize fleeting pleasures, not fulfillment. That's why companies release a new phone every year, even when the old one works perfectly well. That's why fashion cycles shift long before our clothes wear out. Short bursts of excitement drive consumption; quiet contentment does not. Fleeting pleasure feeds the market, while fulfillment feeds the soul.

To live well, we don't need to eliminate fleeting pleasures altogether. Life is meant to be enjoyed. Buying a treat, celebrating a milestone, or upgrading something that genuinely improves life can all be part of happiness. But the key is not to mistake fleeting pleasure for lasting fulfillment. When we rely solely on quick highs, we remain stuck in the cycle of craving. When we cultivate fulfillment, our happiness becomes steady and resilient.

I remember a period when I was constantly upgrading the little things in my life — a better coffee maker, a sleeker phone, a newer laptop. Each purchase came with the promise of ease, efficiency, or a bit of extra happiness. And for a short while, it worked. I felt proud setting up the new gadget, excited to show it off, even convinced that I had improved my life. But within weeks, the glow faded.

The shiny object became background noise, no more magical than the one it replaced. Soon, I was browsing for the next upgrade, repeating the cycle.

Contrast that with another memory: sitting on a porch one summer evening with a close friend. We weren't doing anything extraordinary — just talking, watching the sky shift from orange to deep blue, listening to crickets in the grass. The conversation wandered from serious topics to laughter and back again. That night cost nothing. There was no novelty, no upgrade, no purchase to validate it. And yet, years later, I can recall the feeling with perfect clarity: warmth, connection, peace. That memory still nourishes me. It gave fulfillment, not just pleasure.

This is the power of presence. When we are fully engaged in a moment, even the simplest experiences expand in richness. A meal becomes more than food; it becomes connection. A walk becomes more than exercise; it becomes discovery. A conversation becomes more than words; it becomes belonging. These experiences don't fade as quickly as purchases do. They weave themselves into the fabric of who we are.

The challenge, of course, is that the world is not

designed to make noticing easy. We are constantly distracted, nudged toward craving the next thing instead of appreciating what is already here. That's why we need small, practical ways to train our attention back toward fulfillment.

One simple tool is a contentment journal. At the end of each day, write down three moments when you felt genuinely at ease or grateful. Not when you felt excited or entertained — but when you felt quietly satisfied. It could be the way the morning light came through your window, the laughter of a coworker, or the satisfaction of finishing a task. Over time, this practice rewires the brain to notice and savor fulfillment rather than overlook it.

Another exercise is what I call the "enough question." The next time you feel the urge to buy something new or chase another milestone, pause and ask: What do I already have that meets this need? If you're tempted by new shoes, ask whether your old ones still work. If the answer is yes, maybe the deeper need isn't footwear but novelty, variety, or even a spark of joy. Could that need be met in another way — a new recipe, a walk in a different neighborhood, or starting a fresh conversation?

These practices don't forbid ambition or pleasure.

They simply slow the cycle long enough to give you a choice. Instead of being pulled along by the current of "more," you get to ask: Is this necessary? Will this bring fleeting pleasure, or lasting fulfillment?

Redefining happiness isn't about rejecting pleasure altogether. It's about refusing to confuse the sugar rush of novelty with the nourishment of true fulfillment. The first bite of cake is delightful; living on cake alone leaves us sick. Similarly, the thrill of a new purchase is fine in small doses, but if it becomes our main diet of happiness, we'll always be chasing and never arriving.

Fulfillment requires something different: attention, presence, and gratitude. And when we choose it consistently, something remarkable happens — we stop living at the mercy of circumstances. Happiness becomes less fragile, less dependent on the next raise, the next vacation, the next gadget. It becomes something we carry with us, a lens we choose to wear.

Psychologists call this shift internalizing the source of well-being. Instead of waiting for outside events to determine our mood, we cultivate practices that anchor us. Gratitude pauses, daily reflections, moments of silence — these are like stakes in the ground that keep us steady when life's winds blow. Over time, resilience grows. When hardships come, as they inevitably will, we don't collapse as easily. We have already trained ourselves to look for light, even when shadows stretch long.

Community plays a powerful role in this. Alone, it is easy to forget our own values and slip back into chasing. Surrounded by others who equate happiness with accumulation, we feel pressure to conform. But with even a small circle of people who share a different vision — friends who celebrate presence over possessions, who measure success in experiences rather than square footage — we feel permission to live differently.

A conversation with a supportive friend can be enough to reset our perspective. Where social media might fuel envy, real connection can fuel gratitude. Where advertising says buy this to feel worthy, a trusted voice can remind us, you are already enough. We borrow each other's light in moments when our own feels dim.

This is why building rhythms of community matters. A weekly dinner, a shared walk, a group that talks about what they're grateful for — these simple practices reinforce fulfillment. They remind us that joy is multiplied in company, and that meaning is often found in the bonds between us rather than the objects around us.

Reflection is another key to sustaining joy. Every so often, pause and ask: How does my life feel with these habits in place? Am I calmer? More present? Less restless? Without reflection, habits can slide into routine, losing their power. With reflection, they become reminders of growth. You realize that the urge to chase is quieter, that you laugh more easily, that you notice things you once overlooked.

And finally, sustaining happiness requires grace. Some days, you will slip back into old patterns. You'll chase approval, buy something you don't need, scroll endlessly in search of distraction. That's not failure; it's being human. The key is not perfection but persistence. Forgive yourself quickly, and begin again. The sun rises every day — and so can you.

By now it's clear: happiness is not a destination on the horizon. It is a way of seeing, a posture of the heart. We cannot control every circumstance — illness will come, losses will sting, uncertainty will linger — but we can choose how we orient ourselves toward those realities. This is why happiness is better understood not as a mood that drifts in and out, but as a mindset we can cultivate.

A mindset doesn't mean forced cheer or denial of pain. It means balance. It means noticing sorrow without letting it dominate the whole story, acknowledging stress without forgetting gratitude, admitting imperfection while still choosing joy. Over time, this balance strengthens like a muscle. Each time we pause for gratitude, or choose fulfillment over distraction, we reinforce a pattern. Eventually, that pattern becomes our default way of moving through the world.

Think of it like light breaking through clouds. A single beam may not change the weather, but it changes how we experience the day. With practice, we stop waiting for clear skies to feel light; we learn to notice it even in stormy seasons. This is the quiet resilience of a happiness mindset.

Sharing is part of this transformation. Joy that remains private tends to fade, but joy that is given away multiplies. A kind word, a small gesture, a patient response — these ripple outward. Neuroscience confirms what we already feel instinctively: kindness boosts the giver's well-being as much as the receiver's. Sunshine spreads when we let it spill into someone else's life.

The shift comes when happiness is no longer treated as a special project, reserved for rituals or journals, but allowed to infuse the ordinary. It belongs in the way you sip your coffee slowly instead of rushing. It lives in listening fully when a child tells a story, even if you've heard it before. It emerges when you step outside for a breath between tasks, or laugh freely with a friend. Sunshine isn't a separate practice — it's a way of inhabiting daily life.

Seen this way, happiness is not fragile. It doesn't vanish when circumstances wobble. It weaves itself into the fabric of ordinary days until it becomes second nature. This is not about lowering the bar or settling for less; it is about removing the blindfold. It is about realizing that joy was never far away — it was hidden in the details we overlooked.

Of course, growth still matters. We are meant to learn, to stretch, to aspire. But there is a difference between growth rooted in curiosity and growth driven by inadequacy. When we chase because we believe we're not enough, we exhaust ourselves. When we grow because life is full and we want to experience it more deeply, even the striving feels joyful. That is the paradox: when you stop needing growth to prove your worth, you discover growth becomes richer.

As this chapter closes, one truth remains: happiness isn't earned later, it's practiced now. And the more we practice, the more we see.

Redefining happiness is really about reclaiming authorship. For too long, many of us have allowed corporations, advertisements, and social pressures to script what should make us happy. They tell us it is the promotion, the bigger house, the sleeker phone, the curated image. But when we look honestly, most of those prescriptions leave us restless.

Taking back authorship means asking a new question: What truly matters to me? For some, the answer will be fewer possessions but richer experiences. For others, it might be choosing time over money, or presence over productivity. There is no single formula. What matters is that the answer belongs to you.

This act of reclaiming is rarely easy. Our culture does not often celebrate "enough." It celebrates "more." So there may be resistance — from coworkers who measure worth in promotions, from friends who equate fun with consumption, even from parts of yourself conditioned to want more. But every time you choose fulfillment over fleeting pleasure, presence over accumulation, you are quietly stepping out of that system. You are writing a different story.

And here's the beautiful irony: once you stop chasing "more," you actually see more. Sunshine shows up in places you once overlooked. You measure your life not by what you can add, but by how deeply you can live. Joy becomes less a prize to win and more a practice of paying attention.

That practice doesn't require perfection. You don't have to glow with gratitude every moment or resist every consumer urge. You only need to notice. To pause. To ask the "enough question" when temptation arises. To choose fulfillment whenever you can. These small acts, repeated, build a life that feels lighter, calmer, and more your own.

Think of today. Were there moments of quiet joy you might have missed? The taste of your coffee, the sound of laughter, the way sunlight spilled across your floor. These are not grand or expensive, yet they sustain us far longer than purchases ever do. This is the essence of redefined happiness: not constant elation, but the steady recognition that light is always within reach.

As we move forward, the next step is to understand why the old story — the story of more — became so dominant in the first place. Why has a culture of accumulation and comparison come to feel so natural that we hardly question it? Why does the corporate world profit from keeping us perpetually unsatisfied? How has advertising become so skilled at manufacturing desire, and why do we continue to measure progress by the sheer volume of what we can add?

These questions matter, because once we see the system clearly, we are far less likely to be trapped by it. Chapter 2, The Myth of More, will take us behind the curtain, examining how the culture of excess took root and why it persists. Only by understanding the myth can we begin to free ourselves from it.

For now, hold this truth close: happiness is not postponed, not purchased, not promised by the next milestone. It is practiced in the present, noticed in the ordinary, and sustained by gratitude. It is not about adding more, but about recognizing enough. And in a world forever shouting for more, that recognition is nothing short of revolutionary.

CHAPTER TWO

THE MYTH OF MORE

To understand why contentment feels elusive, we have to face the story we've been told our entire lives: the myth of more.

The myth insists that happiness is always one rung above where we stand. Life is presented as a ladder, our worth measured by how high we climb. Work harder, earn more, buy better, achieve greater — only then, it promises, will we arrive.

It's a seductive story because it's wrapped in images of success. We admire the people who appear to have "made it," who glide through life without limits. We conflate material abundance with emotional satisfaction. And because there is always someone above us on that ladder, the myth never runs out of fuel. There's always another level, another title, another possession.

But the myth has no finish line. Even those we imagine as successful often admit to feeling restless, pressured, incomplete. If "more" truly led to fulfillment, wouldn't the wealthiest and most powerful also be the most at peace? Yet study after study shows the opposite: beyond a certain point, money stops moving the needle on happiness.

So why do we keep believing?

Part of the answer lies in the culture of corporate growth. Businesses survive by selling, and to keep growing they need us to keep buying. True satisfaction would dry up demand. So dissatisfaction gets sold back to us as aspiration. Commercials rarely show people who are simply content; they show the glow of acquisition, the rush of novelty. The message is constant: you are one purchase away from happiness.

The glow fades quickly, and another product waits. New season, new model, new trend. The cycle is not designed to be fulfilled — it is designed to keep us moving. Growth is built into the DNA of the system, and contentment is treated as a threat. A company that encouraged "enough" would soon collapse. And so we live in a world where consumption is duty, and sufficiency feels like failure.

The myth doesn't just live in ads and products. It seeps into our workplaces and personal identities. In most companies, "growth" is the only tense that matters: quarterly earnings must beat last quarter's, sales must rise, productivity must accelerate. Even when profits are healthy, if they are not higher than before, they are called failure. The same logic shapes careers: employees who perform well but not better than last year are labeled stagnant.

This mindset migrates inward. Our value becomes linked to constant improvement. A job title isn't enough unless it leads to another. A hobby doesn't count unless it is monetized or tracked. Rest looks suspiciously like regression. Even friendships are framed in terms of utility — are they expanding our network, opening doors, improving us? The myth of more quietly converts every dimension of life into a race of endless escalation.

The myth of more is powerful because it doesn't simply describe our world — it shapes it. We don't just hear the story in commercials; we live inside it. To see it clearly, we need to understand how it operates on both our instincts and our environment.

Advertising is the myth's loudest storyteller. On the surface, it shows us products. Beneath the surface, it manufactures desire. Its most effective message isn't "Here's what's for sale," but "What you already have is inadequate." The whisper is steady: you are incomplete.

Think of the slogans that have surrounded us: Because you're worth it. Have it your way. The ultimate driving machine. These don't just promote shampoo, hamburgers, or cars — they promote identity. They suggest that dignity, belonging, and joy can be bought. If they can be bought, they can also be withheld until we spend.

The trick works because it taps into natural longings. We want to be respected, attractive, loved, successful. There is nothing wrong with those desires. But advertising hijacks them, attaching them to products that cannot possibly deliver. A phone can't guarantee connection. A luxury bag can't secure respect. A car can't provide love. Yet the images are stitched so tightly together that the illusion feels real.

Even more subtly, advertising normalizes excess. Commercials rarely display one thing; they display abundance — closets overflowing, tables stacked, pantries gleaming. The lesson is that "more" is the baseline. If your life doesn't look like this, it must be lacking. And because the images surround us daily, they slip under our defenses. We stop questioning them. Soon the desires they plant feel like our own thoughts.

Social media has amplified this to exhausting levels. Platforms designed for connection often function as stages for comparison. We scroll through curated images of other people's vacations, promotions, and purchases, and measure ourselves against them. Private joys become public performances, validated only by likes. It's not enough to enjoy a meal; it must be documented. Not enough to rest; it must look productive. The myth thrives in these feeds, convincing us we are always a few steps behind.

And the cost is not just psychological — it is

practical. Walk into a superstore and the myth is on every shelf. Twelve-packs, seasonal resets, aisles of cheap goods designed to be replaced quickly. The promise is convenience; the reality is disposability. A shirt cheaper than lunch lasts only a season. Shoes wear out, toasters fail, fashions cycle, closets swell. We buy more, but satisfaction stays thin.

This culture of disposability shifts how we see the world. If everything can be replaced, nothing feels precious. Objects, time, even relationships begin to feel temporary, exchangeable, optional. And while corporations profit brilliantly from this churn, individuals pay dearly. This culture of disposability doesn't just fill shelves; it reshapes expectations. When everything is made to be replaced, we stop expecting durability — from objects, from experiences, even from commitments. Studies confirm what we sense: crowded spaces increase stress and drain focus. The very things we hoped would simplify life end up suffocating it.

Debt is another cost. Even when items are inexpensive, the cycle of constant replacement adds up. Credit cards and buy-now-pay-later plans whisper that joy can be immediate while responsibility can be delayed. But the bill always arrives. What felt like progress turns into a weight that lingers long after the thrill has faded. Many households live in quiet tension — stretching to keep pace with an imagined standard of "enough" that never actually arrives.

There is also fatigue — not just financial, but emotional. Each new purchase requires storage, cleaning, organizing, and maintenance. Each new responsibility at work demands more hours, more energy, more attention. "More" always carries hidden costs. Over time, those costs crowd out what we value most: time with loved ones, moments of rest, energy for creativity. The treadmill keeps moving, and exhaustion follows.

The myth works so well because it targets our psychology. It preys on three powerful instincts: fear, insecurity, and belonging.

Fear is the oldest. We are wired to notice when others have something we don't. Thousands of years ago, that vigilance meant survival. Today, advertising and social media exploit it, whispering: If you don't buy this, you'll fall behind. If you don't climb, you'll be irrelevant. The fear of being left out keeps us sprinting.

Insecurity is the second lever. We all carry private doubts: Am I good enough? Do I measure up? The myth doesn't soothe these doubts; it amplifies them. It suggests that maybe we aren't enough — but we could be, with the right clothes, house, job title. "More" becomes a proposed cure for inadequacy. But because no purchase erases insecurity, the cycle continues.

Belonging is the final hook. We crave acceptance and connection. The myth sells products as passports into identity groups: the tribe with the latest phone, the class represented by a car, the lifestyle symbolized by a brand. But belonging bought this way is fragile. When the product ages, so does the status. True belonging can't be swiped at a checkout.

The tragedy is that in chasing more, we often miss the value of what we already have. When "more" is the measure, sufficiency looks like failure. Stability feels like stagnation. Contentment feels like settling. Yet life is not a ladder meant to be climbed endlessly. It is a garden to be tended. A garden doesn't expand by racing upward; it flourishes through care, patience, and balance. Growth happens, but it is cyclical, sustainable, and rooted.

Naming the myth for what it is — a story

designed to keep us restless — is the first step in reclaiming our perspective. Only then can we begin asking the better question: not "How do I get more?" but "What is truly enough?"

The myth of more is persuasive because it disguises itself as progress. We all want to move forward, to become wiser, stronger, better versions of ourselves. Growth is a natural human desire. But the myth hijacks that instinct, reducing progress to accumulation. A faster phone is framed as advancement. A bigger house is celebrated as proof of success. A higher title is treated as a mark of worth. Yet these markers rarely deliver what they promise.

A colleague once shared how she turned down a promotion that would have doubled her salary but demanded sixty-hour weeks and constant travel. Her peers were stunned. Why would anyone refuse "progress"? She simply smiled and said, "Because I already have enough. I'd rather have my evenings back." For her, progress wasn't about climbing higher; it was about reclaiming time, health, and joy.

That choice illustrates the deeper truth: real progress is personal, not universal. It can't be measured by a ladder everyone climbs in lockstep. Sometimes the greatest step forward is choosing not to move at all. Sometimes it is tending the garden we already have instead of chasing another plot of land.

Awareness is the first tool for stepping off the treadmill. The myth of more thrives on autopilot — the constant reflex to reach for the next thing without asking why. Pausing to notice weakens its grip. The next time you feel an urge to upgrade, ask: Am I buying an object or chasing a feeling? When you feel restless at work, ask: Is this about growth I value, or growth I've been told to want? When you catch yourself comparing your life to someone else's, ask: Am I measuring myself against their "more" instead of my own enough?

These questions won't always lead to easy answers, but they create space. And in that space lives choice. Choice is what the myth of more quietly takes from us — the choice to say no, to step aside, to define success differently.

Reflection is another tool. Look back on the last time you bought something you thought would change your life. How long did the thrill last? Did the purchase bring lasting fulfillment, or did it fade into the background? What about the last time you said yes to more responsibility — did it deepen your life, or drain it? These aren't questions for guilt, but for clarity. Over time, they reveal the pattern: "more" rarely delivers on its promises.

The system around us won't stop selling. Corporations will keep equating joy with products. Workplaces will continue rewarding escalation. Social media will keep parading curated lives. But once we see the myth for what it is, we are no longer captive. We can choose when to engage, when to resist, and when to declare, quietly but firmly, that what we already have is enough.

The myth of more tells us we must climb faster, consume more, never rest. But here is the truth: you are not behind. You are not lacking. You are not incomplete. Happiness isn't waiting at the next rung of the ladder. It is already present, rooted in the garden of your life.

In the next chapter, we will slow the myth's storyteller to a crawl: advertising. We'll look closely at how it works, why it is so persuasive, and how to recognize when it's shaping your desires. Because once you see the story being told, you can decide whether to keep listening.

CHAPTER THREE:

ADVERTISING THE DREAM

If the myth of more is the story, then advertising is its greatest storyteller. No other force has shaped our sense of happiness more directly. Ads don't just sell products — they sell identities, lifestyles, and dreams. And they do it so seamlessly that we often don't notice.

From jingles we memorized as kids to the glossy images on our phones today, advertising has always delivered the same message: your life is fine, but it could be better. This cereal will make mornings brighter. This shampoo will make you confident. This car will make you free. The product is secondary. What's really for sale is the feeling of being more complete.

This approach is powerful because it bypasses logic and goes straight to emotion. Nobody literally believes that a soda will make them adventurous or that sneakers guarantee belonging. But when we see smiling faces, perfect families, or stylish athletes, our subconscious fills in the blanks. The product becomes shorthand for joy, connection, and identity. The promise is never, buy this thing. The promise is, buy the life that comes with it.

Advertising's brilliance lies in its subtlety. Commercials rarely argue. They suggest. They create a whisper of dissatisfaction: maybe what you have isn't enough. Multiply that whisper by thousands of impressions a day and it stops feeling like persuasion. It feels like reality.

And advertising isn't confined to TV breaks anymore. It's woven into our routines. Billboards on the commute. Banners in search engines. Sponsored posts hidden among friends' photos.

Elevators, gas pumps, even bathroom stalls carry messages. Ads are no longer interruptions — they're the background hum of daily life. That constant drip shapes desires before we even recognize them as desires.

The most effective ads don't create needs; they hijack them. Love, respect, freedom, security — these are deeply human longings. A perfume ad doesn't talk about ingredients; it shows romance. A car ad doesn't dwell on horsepower; it shows a lone driver on an open road. Sneakers aren't sold as shoes but as symbols of grit and identity. By tying products to universal desires, ads convince us that the only way to meet them is through consumption.

But here's the catch: no purchase can actually deliver love, respect, or freedom. At best, it delivers a momentary thrill. When the feeling fades, another ad waits with another promise. The cycle feeds itself endlessly.

Every word, image, and color in advertising is chosen for psychological impact. The goal is not to inform but to persuade, often bypassing logic altogether. Scarcity, association, repetition, aspiration, comparison — these are the quiet tools that make ads effective. And because they're so familiar, we often don't see them for what they are: deliberate strategies to keep us reaching.

Advertising thrives because it knows how to work with our psychology, not against it. It doesn't need to present facts or evidence. It only needs to strike chords that already exist within us. Over time, these tactics become so familiar that we barely notice them — and that is precisely why they work.

One of the oldest tricks is scarcity. A banner that says "limited time only" or "while supplies last" flips a switch deep in our brains. When something seems rare, we automatically assign it more value. Scarcity makes us imagine regret — the feeling of missing out — and so we act quickly to avoid it. The irony is that most of these products aren't rare at all. Scarcity is manufactured, a clever illusion designed to turn hesitation into urgency.

Another tool is association. Products are linked with feelings we all desire: freedom, love, beauty, strength. A sports car commercial doesn't focus on engineering specs; it shows a driver racing into a blazing sunset, wind in their hair, the road wide open. The car isn't just selling speed — it's selling liberation. A shampoo ad doesn't highlight chemicals or nutrients; it shows flirtation, confidence, joy. The bottle becomes a proxy for human connection. The message is clear: if you want the feeling, you need the product.

Then there is repetition. Psychologists call it the "mere exposure effect." The more often we see or hear something, the more familiar and trustworthy it feels. This is why jingles burrow into our heads, and why logos appear on everything from stadiums to pens. Repetition doesn't prove a product's value — it makes it feel like truth simply by echo.

Aspiration is another subtle but powerful lever. Advertising rarely speaks to who we are today. Instead, it paints a picture of who we could be. It shows us the future self — fitter, more confident, more admired — and then quietly offers the product as the bridge to becoming that person. Social media has made this tactic even more persuasive. Influencers blur the line between lifestyle and marketing, weaving products into their daily routines. We don't just admire their lives; we begin to believe their possessions are what made those lives possible.

Finally, there is comparison. Ads often rely on showing us people who look just a little better than we feel. The smiling neighbor with the perfect lawn. The polished colleague with the stylish outfit. The laughing family at the dinner table. No words are necessary. The message lands: they have something you don't. If you want to catch up, here's what you need to buy.

Individually, each tactic may feel harmless — even clever. Together, they create an ecosystem where desire is never fully satisfied, because it was never meant to be. Advertising doesn't only persuade us to buy; it fosters a worldview: happiness is external, and it's always one purchase away. Once we adopt that worldview, every ad has fertile ground in which to grow.

Some of the clearest examples of advertising's power come from the brands that built empires on stories rather than products.

Take Coca-Cola. For decades, its commercials have rarely been about the drink itself. They've been about friendship, laughter, and joy. A bottle of soda is framed as the key to connection. The liquid is almost incidental; what you're really buying is belonging.

Apple takes a different route. Its ads rarely talk about technical details. Instead, they present sleek designs and minimalist images that whisper individuality and creativity. To own an iPhone isn't just to have a phone — it's to be different, smarter, and more original than the rest.

Nike built its dominance not by emphasizing rubber soles but by attaching its shoes to achievement and grit. "Just Do It" isn't a description of footwear; it's a philosophy of life. The swoosh isn't fabric — it's perseverance.

These aren't campaigns. They are cultural narratives. They don't just reflect values; they shape them. Over time, we begin to think of joy as a Coke, creativity as an Apple, perseverance as a Nike. Slowly, our vocabulary for happiness and identity gets outsourced to brands.

This is where advertising becomes most powerful: not when it convinces us to buy one thing, but when it convinces us to buy into a worldview. A furniture ad isn't just about couches — it's about what a "happy family" should look like. A car gliding through mountains doesn't just sell horsepower — it sells the fantasy of freedom, even if most of us drive in traffic. Ads define success as aspiration, and aspiration by definition can never be fully reached.

The rise of influencer marketing has blurred the

line even further. Instead of polished commercials, we see peers and celebrities weaving products into their daily routines. A "morning routine" video doubles as a commercial for skincare, supplements, and gadgets. A travel blogger's photo of a sunset beach is also a subtle promotion for airlines or resorts. The genius lies in the delivery: we don't feel like we're being sold to; we feel like we're being let in. Yet the underlying message remains the same — happiness looks like this, and to have it, you need to buy what I buy.

So how do we resist? The first step is awareness — noticing the story being told. The next time an ad hooks you, pause and ask: What emotion is this selling me? Can this product actually deliver that? Do I want the item, or the lifestyle it's attached to? Often, the promise and the product don't match. A vacation can provide rest, but not lasting peace. A designer bag may boost confidence briefly, but it can't secure belonging. By separating the object from the story, we weaken advertising's spell.

The real danger isn't that ads waste our money — it's that they shrink our imagination. When joy is consistently depicted as something you can buy, we forget to dream of joy that is free. And that narrowing of possibility shapes not only individuals, but entire cultures.

The costs of advertising run deeper than the dollars we spend. They touch our homes, our peace of mind, and even the way our children grow up.

One cost is waste. When ads convince us that last year's phone, last season's jacket, or last decade's furniture are "outdated," perfectly useful items get discarded. Landfills overflow with yesterday's purchases, while factories churn out tomorrow's at ever faster rates. The cycle of advertising and consumption isn't just personal habit — it's industrial machinery, driving waste on a global scale. But because ads keep our eyes fixed on the next purchase, we rarely notice the trail left behind.

Another cost is stress — not from the possessions themselves, but from the constant pressure to acquire more. Studies show that heavy exposure to advertising inflates material aspirations: the more ads we see, the more we believe we lack. The "needs" list grows faster than paychecks can keep up, creating a low-grade anxiety that hums beneath daily life. A jingle, a billboard, a social post — each one tugs at our sense of adequacy. Over time, these messages don't just suggest we buy more; they quietly convince us we are less until we do.

Perhaps the most troubling cost is the way advertising shapes the youngest minds. Children see between 20,000 and 40,000 commercials a year, and most are not designed to inform but to embed emotions. Mascots aren't just characters; they become companions. Cartoon breaks slide seamlessly into toy promotions, where "fun" is equated with ownership. Apps aimed at kids often smuggle in product placements so subtly that play and consumption blur into the same activity. Long before they can spell the word advertisement, children have learned its lesson: joy comes with a price tag.

This early conditioning plants seeds that grow quietly. A child who learns that belonging comes from having the right sneakers or the newest game carries that association into adolescence and beyond. The worldview advertising instills is not about one toy or one snack — it's about wiring desire itself. By the time these children reach adulthood, they aren't just consumers of products; they are consumers of identities. And because those identities are tied to possessions, the hunger rarely ends.

So how do we defend ourselves? Not by fleeing every billboard or deleting every app, but by learning to see ads clearly. Awareness is the first defense. The next time you encounter one, don't absorb it passively. Ask: What story is this ad telling? What emotion is it trying to spark? A glossy car commercial isn't about freedom; it's about profit. A fast-food jingle isn't about joy; it's about sales. When we expose the trick, the illusion weakens.

The second defense is boundaries. Turn off targeted ad tracking, unsubscribe from promotional emails, reduce time on platforms designed to monetize attention. Even small changes create breathing room. Over time, you may notice fewer restless urges, fewer moments of sudden dissatisfaction.

The third defense is defining success for yourself. If advertising thrives on telling us what to want, then one of the most radical acts is to write our own script. What genuinely brings you fulfillment? Keep those answers close. When ads try to sell a different story, compare it with your own. If it doesn't align, let it pass.

Gratitude is the final tool. Ads fix our gaze on

what's missing. Gratitude shifts it to what's already here. Each day, noting even one or two simple things — a good meal, a kind gesture, a moment of rest — builds resilience against the constant whisper that you need more.

Advertising will keep insisting you're incomplete. But with awareness, boundaries, and gratitude, you can stop listening. You can reclaim your attention — and with it, your freedom.

Advertising doesn't just shape individuals — it reshapes entire cultures. Over time, the stories told in commercials become the stories societies tell themselves. They create norms, expectations, and shared visions of what a "good life" should look like.

Consider the American Dream. For decades, it has been symbolized by the house with a white picket fence, two cars in the driveway, and a neatly trimmed lawn. That image didn't emerge from philosophy textbooks or political speeches. It was fueled by advertising and marketing campaigns after World War II, when corporations needed to sell homes, cars, and appliances to a booming middle class. The dream of ownership became the dream of citizenship. To be successful wasn't simply to be free; it was to buy.

Other cultures absorbed similar scripts. Luxury brands are marketed worldwide as markers of identity and status, transforming handbags, watches, and shoes into signals of worth. Tourism campaigns sell not just destinations but lifestyles — convincing us that travel only counts if it looks like the brochure. Even holidays have been rewritten. Valentine's Day, once about handwritten notes and simple gestures, now centers on diamonds, roses, and extravagant dinners. Christmas has become as much about shopping malls as sacred rituals.

When advertising sets the cultural standard, sufficiency looks like failure. Abundance is normal. Simplicity is suspect. We learn to equate possessions with pride and consumption with celebration. These scripts are so pervasive that we often repeat them without realizing they originated in a boardroom.

But culture is not fixed. Just as advertising has built one story, we can build another. Around the world, counter-movements are rising: minimalism, slow living, voluntary simplicity. These philosophies challenge the assumption that more is better, suggesting instead that happiness often grows when we pare back. Fewer possessions, less media, fewer hours at work — these choices create space to rediscover what matters. They are small rebellions against the advertising machine, reminders that culture is shaped not only by corporations but also by individuals making different choices.

The real danger of advertising culture isn't only that it drains wallets or fills landfills. It narrows imagination. When joy is consistently depicted as a purchase — the latest gadget, the biggest home, the perfect vacation — we forget to envision joy rooted in meaning, connection, and presence. Advertising offers one narrow definition of happiness: the shiny, purchased kind. If we aren't careful, we accept it as the only one.

But other visions are possible. We can imagine a culture where relationships matter more than retail, where worth is measured in kindness rather than consumption, where communities flourish through presence rather than possessions. These aren't fantasies — they are choices waiting for us to make them.

In the end, advertising's greatest trick is its whisper: You are incomplete, but you could be whole if you buy. Once we recognize the formula, its power fades. We begin to see that our deepest longings — for connection, freedom, belonging, peace — cannot be purchased. They can only be cultivated.

And yet, even when we reject the story, its residue lingers. Every "more" we've bought eventually lands somewhere — on a shelf, in a closet, in the background of our lives. This is the quiet aftermath that advertising never shows: the weight of excess. That is where we turn next.

CHAPTER FOUR

THE WEIGHT OF EXCESS

At first, "more" feels like freedom. More options, more purchases, more choices. But over time, more becomes a weight. What begins as abundance turns into clutter, debt, and distraction. The very things we hoped would bring joy often leave us feeling heavier.

Walk into a typical home today and you'll see the evidence. Closets crammed with clothes, many of them barely worn. Kitchen drawers stuffed with gadgets bought on impulse. Shelves lined with unread books, unused electronics, decorations once exciting now gathering dust. Garages meant for cars filled with boxes. We don't simply live with enough — we drown in excess.

This has become so normal that we barely notice. We justify it with excuses: It might come in handy someday. I'm just being prepared. But beneath those stories lies a quieter truth: much of what we hold onto doesn't serve us. It takes up space, demands attention, and quietly erodes our peace of mind.

THE HIDDEN COSTS

The impact of excess extends beyond feelings. It shows up in ledgers, calendars, and lost chances.

Financial cost. Every object represents a transaction, a trade of time for money and money for stuff. Individually, purchases seem harmless; together, they swell into debt. Studies show that the average American household carries more than $6,000 in credit card debt, much of it tied to consumer spending rather than necessity. Storage has become a booming business — the U.S. now has over 50,000 self-storage facilities, more than McDonald's and Starbucks combined. The promise of freedom through ownership too often becomes bondage to payments and monthly rental fees for things we rarely use.

Time cost. Objects are not passive. They require cleaning, storing, fixing, or replacing. Research estimates that the average person spends 2.5 days per year looking for misplaced items, and American families devote 8 hours a week on household cleaning and maintenance. A house filled with possessions quietly drafts us into service. Weekends become maintenance shifts. Free hours, scarce to begin with, are consumed by caretaking for things.

Opportunity cost. The heaviest toll is unseen. Surveys reveal that over half of homeowners say they don't use at least one room in their house regularly, often because it's been overtaken by clutter. Money spent on excess goods is money not spent on experiences that create lasting meaning — travel, learning, or time with others. Research from Cornell University found that people derive greater and longer-lasting happiness from experiences than from material purchases. Time swallowed by upkeep is time not poured into relationships or creative work. The hidden price of excess is the future it silently steals.

This is the full weight of ownership: not just what something costs at the store, but what it continues to cost long after the receipt fades.

THE PSYCHOLOGY OF EXCESS

Psychologists have long studied why clutter and excess weigh so heavily on us. One key factor is cognitive load — the brain's limit on how much information it can comfortably process at once. Each visible object, whether useful or not, registers as data that the mind must sort, store, or dismiss. A well-known 1990s study by John Sweller on cognitive load theory showed that when working memory is overwhelmed, learning and decision-making collapse. The same principle applies at home: a cluttered room doesn't just crowd the eye; it bombards the mind, forcing it to filter constantly. Neuroscientists at Princeton University found that people working in messy environments had reduced ability to focus and process information, because the visual chaos directly competed for neural resources. This is why even sitting still in a messy space can feel tiring — your brain is doing background labor.

Excess also fuels decision fatigue. Every added option — which shirt to wear, which mug to use, which gadget to try — demands mental energy. Social psychologist Roy Baumeister's research on ego depletion demonstrates that willpower is a finite resource: the more small choices we make, the less mental stamina we have left for significant ones. One famous field study of judges showed that parole decisions were far more favorable earlier in the day, when decision fatigue had not yet set in. Translated into daily life, clutter isn't neutral; it drains the very resource we rely on for focus and self-control.

Then there's the dopamine cycle of consumption. Neuroscientists know that the act of anticipating and making a purchase triggers the brain's reward system, releasing a small burst of dopamine. This chemical "reward" feels good in the moment, but the effect fades quickly. The brain then craves the next hit, keeping us trapped in a loop of acquisition.

Researchers at Stanford University have shown that novelty itself — not ownership — drives much of the dopamine response. That's why packages on the doorstep feel exciting, even if what's inside loses its appeal within days. The result is a home crowded not with carefully chosen essentials, but with artifacts of fleeting impulses.

Excess is not just physical — it is neurological. It reshapes our habits, depletes our attention, and wires us into cycles of craving that clutter both our homes and our minds. Left unchecked, the psychology of excess ensures that we remain restless, not because we lack, but because we are overwhelmed by what we already have. If psychology explains why we keep accumulating, the illusion of control explains why we defend it.

THE ILLUSION OF CONTROL

Part of the reason we accumulate is the belief that possessions equal preparedness. We buy extra clothes just in case, stockpile gadgets for situations that never arrive, or hold onto items because someday they might be useful. It feels like security.

But this sense of control is often an illusion. The tool we think will solve a problem sits untouched in a drawer. The backup appliance breaks before we use it. The mountain of "someday" supplies becomes clutter long before it becomes helpful. Instead of protecting us, the stockpile makes us anxious — a visual reminder of imagined problems we may never face.

Real security doesn't come from unlimited things. It comes from flexibility, creativity, and relationships. The neighbor who lends us a ladder, the skill of improvising with what we already have, the trust that we can solve problems as they arise — these provide more stability than garages and attics packed with just-in-case objects. Excess convinces us we're safer, but often we're only heavier.

Excess doesn't just crowd our homes; it crowds our relationships. Many arguments begin with stuff. Couples spar over money spent on gadgets. Parents and children fight over toys or devices. Siblings dispute over estates. Possessions that once promised joy often become sources of conflict.

Even when they don't cause outright fights, they shift our focus. A guest spills wine on a new rug, and instead of enjoying their company, we fixate on the stain. A child breaks a decoration, and instead of laughing it off, we mourn the object more than we celebrate the moment. Slowly, things take priority over people. Attention drifts from connection to protection.

Possessions also whisper guilt. The exercise bike in the corner isn't just metal; it's a reminder of goals never met. The pile of unread books isn't just paper; it's evidence of time never found. Craft supplies hint at ambitions left unfinished. Objects don't sit silently — they speak, and often what they say discourages us.

Over time, our very identity can become tangled in what we own. Clothes become proof of taste, cars status symbols, homes showpieces. But things break. They go out of style. They lose their shine. When worth is tethered to them, self-worth fades along with them.

THE MYTH OF STATUS AND SELF WORTH

Excess doesn't stop at the doorstep. It plays on one of our deepest social instincts: the desire to signal status. Sociologist Thorstein Veblen coined the term conspicuous consumption in the late 19th century to describe purchases made less for utility than for display. The goods have changed — from horse-drawn carriages to luxury SUVs, from parlors to sprawling suburban homes — but the impulse remains. In fact, researchers have found that people often spend more on visible items, like clothing or cars, than on private ones, precisely because they broadcast social standing.

The danger is that this chase quickly becomes a treadmill. There is always someone with a bigger house, a newer phone, a fancier vacation. Social media amplifies this effect: scrolling through curated feeds of highlight reels makes our own lives look smaller in comparison. Psychologists call it the social comparison trap — the tendency to measure ourselves against others. A 2018 study published in Nature Human Behavior found that income comparisons explained more variance in life satisfaction than income itself. In other words, it's not just what we have that matters to our happiness — it's how it stacks up against others. What once felt abundant suddenly feels inadequate.

This isn't just theory; it plays out in daily culture. Entire trends revolve around "haul videos," where influencers proudly display dozens of new outfits, gadgets, or decor items in a single sitting. The appeal isn't in the utility of the purchases, but in the sheer volume — a modern-day performance of abundance. Viewers often report mixed feelings: brief excitement, followed by envy, then the quiet urge to spend in order to keep up. In this way, conspicuous consumption has found its perfect stage — not the carriage ride through town of Veblen's era, but the endless scroll of TikTok, YouTube, and Instagram.

This trap doesn't only distort self-image — it reshapes communities. Neighbors who might have once pooled resources now compete silently through upgrades and additions. The U.S. spends more than $400 billion annually on home improvements, much of it driven not by need but by comparison with others. Conversations drift toward square footage, vacations, and acquisitions rather than meaning or connection. The result is ironic: possessions meant to elevate us often isolate us. Excess, in this sense, overwhelms our capacity for genuine belonging.

And the effects ripple outward. Every purchase has an afterlife. Fast fashion alone produces 92 million tons of textile waste globally each year, and many items end up in landfills or shipped to developing countries, where they overwhelm local economies and ecosystems. Cheap electronics and disposable gadgets leave behind toxic e-waste, with only 20% recycled worldwide. Plastics from packaging and consumer goods fragment into micro-plastics, now found in oceans, soil, drinking water, and even human blood.

The hidden costs are not only environmental but human. Low prices often conceal low wages: the International Labour Organization estimates that 170 million children are engaged in child labor, many in the supply chains of textiles and consumer goods. Factory collapses like the 2013 Rana Plaza disaster in Bangladesh, which killed over 1,100 garment workers, remind us that bargain clothing often comes at a steep human cost. The comforts we chase in the name of security can, in fact, exploit workers and degrade communities far from our sight.

Even neighborhoods change when excess becomes the norm. Instead of borrowing a ladder from next door, we buy duplicates. Instead of sharing tools, toys, or books, we stockpile our own.

This retreat into self-sufficiency weakens community bonds. Yet when neighborhoods embrace sufficiency together — through tool libraries, clothing swaps, repair cafés, or community gardens — something shifts. Possessions stop being measures of status and become resources to share. Sufficiency becomes collective, and belonging returns.

THE TURNNG POINT

For many, the recognition of excess arrives gradually: the frustration of rummaging through clutter, the sting of a credit card bill, the uneasy glance at rooms filled with unused things. Each whisper adds up: Is this really how I want to live?

For others, it comes suddenly: a move, a financial setback, a personal loss. These moments strip away illusions and reveal abundance as burden.

Acknowledging this truth can feel uncomfortable. It means admitting that consumer culture has not delivered. But discomfort opens a doorway. It nudges us to ask: How much is enough? What can I release? What do I actually need to be content?

Change rarely happens overnight. More often, it begins with small steps: donating a bag of clothes, clearing a drawer, choosing not to replace what still works. Each small act of release brings surprising relief. Less isn't a loss — it's a gift.

The joy expands beyond space. Living with less reveals more time, energy, and focus. When possessions no longer overwhelm, we invest in relationships, creativity, and rest. What once looked like subtraction becomes addition — of clarity, purpose, and presence.

It's important to remember that rejecting excess is not the same as rejecting comfort. There is such a thing as a minimal threshold — the baseline of possessions and resources we need to live securely and well. Shelter, clothing, food, warmth, tools for work and creativity: these are not luxuries, but essentials. The problem isn't having them; it's when we continue accumulating far beyond what sustains us.

Psychologists studying happiness consistently find that once basic needs are met, additional possessions contribute very little to well-being. In fact, chasing more often creates more stress than satisfaction. Enough is not about stripping life bare. It's about recognizing when the threshold has already been crossed, and when "more" no longer serves us.

This perspective also protects against the misconception that living with less means deprivation. Minimalism, simplicity, or sufficiency are not about austerity. They are about right-sizing — keeping what adds real value and releasing what doesn't. The minimal threshold frees us to appreciate comfort without tipping into clutter. It reminds us that life's richness doesn't depend on how much we own, but on how well we use and enjoy what we already have.

ENOUGH IS ENOUGH

Living with less doesn't mean deprivation. It means intention. It means keeping what matters and releasing what doesn't. It means refusing to carry the silent weight of excess simply because culture calls it success.

The moment we see excess clearly — not as abundance but as burden — something shifts. We realize that sunshine isn't buried under possessions. It's been here all along, waiting in the space we create when we let go.

The heaviest cost of excess isn't cluttered closets or mounting debt. It's the way it dulls our ability to live fully — keeping us distracted, tired, and restless. But this weight can be lifted. Step by step, piece by piece, we can choose differently.

What's striking is how quickly the benefits appear. A cleared drawer brings space to breathe. A canceled subscription eases stress. Pausing before the next upgrade quiets the mind. Modest choices accumulate into profound freedom.

Perhaps most importantly, stepping away from excess reminds us that we are not defined by what we own. Worth is not measured in square footage, brands, or wardrobes. Our value comes from presence, purpose, and connection — things no store can sell.

And so the question emerges: if more is a burden, what is enough? Where is the line between sufficiency and excess, between joy and distraction, between need and want? These questions are not abstract; they are deeply personal. They form the compass that guides us toward balance.

As we turn to the next chapter, the invitation is clear: begin to explore your own definition of enough. Not the version culture sells, not the standard neighbors chase, but the personal recognition of what sustains without weighing you down. Because once we learn to name enough, we unlock a life that feels lighter, freer, and closer to the sunshine we've been searching for all along.

CHAPTER FIVE
THE POWER OF ENOUGH

What if happiness isn't about reaching for more, but about recognizing when we already have enough? It's a simple question with radical implications. Defining "enough" isn't about settling for less; it's about noticing the moment when our needs are met, our hearts are full, and our lives feel whole.

In a culture that thrives on "more," enough can feel almost rebellious. Companies measure success by perpetual growth. Social media parades lifestyles just out of reach. Even well-meaning friends urge us to keep pushing: earn more, buy more, achieve more. Against that backdrop, declaring that what we already have is sufficient can sound almost heretical.

Modern psychology offers a deeper explanation for why "enough" is so elusive. Researchers call it hedonic adaptation — the tendency of humans to quickly return to a baseline level of happiness, no matter what new thing we acquire. A bigger house, a promotion, or the latest gadget sparks a temporary high, but soon it fades, and we find ourselves wanting again. It's not that we're ungrateful; it's that our brains are wired to normalize gains and move the goalposts.

Related to this is social comparison theory. We rarely measure enough by our own circumstances alone. We measure against neighbors, coworkers, and curated feeds online. Someone else's success shifts our baseline, leaving us restless even when our lives are objectively rich. Psychologists also describe the arrival fallacy: the belief that happiness will finally arrive when we achieve the next milestone. But once we get there, contentment slips away, and a new "arrival" takes its place.

Understanding these traps isn't about shame — it's about awareness. When we recognize that "more" often fails to deliver lasting satisfaction, the idea of enough becomes not only comforting, but liberating. It offers a way out of the cycle.

And yet, think about the moments when you've felt most content. Were they marked by abundance or by sufficiency? Was it the holiday meal with endless courses, or the simple dinner with someone you love? Was it the thrill of a new purchase, or the quiet moment when you realized you needed nothing else to feel whole? Enough isn't deprivation. It's balance instead of excess, peace instead of striving.

Enough is also deeply personal. For one person it may be a modest home and steady work; for another, creative pursuits or travel. The point isn't to adopt someone else's definition, but to craft your own — one rooted in your values rather than society's expectations.

This shift changes everything. Instead of asking How can I get more? we begin to ask What do I truly need to thrive? That reorients decisions about money, possessions, work, and time. It creates boundaries, allows us to say no without guilt, and keeps us from measuring success by someone else's standard.

Choosing enough also takes courage. It means resisting the current that insists we are always behind. It means looking at an ad and saying, I don't need that to be whole. That quiet defiance is transformative.

Enough isn't a finish line we cross once. It's a practice. Each choice becomes an opportunity to ask: Does this add to my life, or is it just more? The more we practice, the stronger the habit becomes — and the lighter life feels.

PRACTICAL WAYS TO DEFINE ENOUGH

A simple place to begin is inventory with intention. Not counting every item, but noticing what adds value. Which belongings bring joy, which feel burdensome? Often a worn chair is more comforting than the expensive one we never sit on.

Another tool is the "enough question." Before buying something, pause: Do I already have something that serves this purpose? That pause shifts us from automatic consumption to thoughtful choice.

Journaling can also clarify sufficiency. List your last five purchases and note how long the satisfaction lasted. Then list five recent experiences — a walk, a meal, a moment of quiet. Compare how long those feelings linger. Most people find experiences leave a deeper imprint than things.

You might also ask: If I lost this tomorrow, would it matter? The answers can be surprising, revealing what truly carries weight.

At a broader level, defining enough requires clarifying values: What do I want more of that money can't buy? Time, peace of mind, creativity, health? Once those values are clear, they act as a compass.

And finally, practice gratitude daily. Gratitude sharpens our sense of sufficiency. Writing down three things each night reminds us that much of what we once longed for is already here.

The pursuit of enough is not a new idea. Across cultures and centuries, wisdom traditions have emphasized sufficiency as the foundation of a good life. The Stoics in ancient Greece taught that virtue and peace come not from abundance but from mastering desire. Epictetus famously said, "Wealth consists not in having great possessions, but in having few wants."

Buddhist teachings echo this through the principle of non-attachment: happiness arises not from clinging to more, but from loosening the grip of craving. In Buddhist practice, sufficiency isn't deprivation — it's freedom from being owned by what we own.

Closer to home, American writers like Henry David Thoreau built their lives around this principle. In Walden, Thoreau chose a small cabin and simple diet not as an act of poverty but as a declaration of independence from society's race for more. His point wasn't that everyone should live in a cabin; it was that living deliberately required knowing when enough had already been reached.

These voices from history remind us that the struggle with "more" is not uniquely modern. What's new is the scale of today's advertising and digital comparison. But the counter-story — that sufficiency brings freedom — has always been with us.

STORIES OF ENOUGH

Sometimes the best way to understand enough is to see it lived out.

I once knew a man who lived in a small apartment above a hardware store. He had only the basics — a table, a couch, shelves of dog-eared novels. He worked part-time, just enough to pay his bills, leaving time for his true passion: painting. His space was modest, but filled with peace and purpose. He often said, "I don't need much. I just need time to paint." That was his enough.

A friend of mine lived the opposite story. She had just bought a sprawling home with new cars and gleaming appliances. From the outside, it looked like abundance. But over coffee she admitted, "I feel like I'm working just to keep up with it all. I wonder if I'm happier than before." Her "more" felt like a treadmill.

Then there was a young couple traveling in a camper van. At first, downsizing was difficult. But over time they felt lighter. "We didn't realize how much energy we spent managing our stuff," they told me. "Now we have less, but more life."

These stories show that enough doesn't have a single shape. For one person, it's time to paint. For another, it's reclaiming peace of mind. For another, it's freedom and togetherness. Enough is always about alignment: ensuring how we live matches what we truly value.

BEYOND POSSESSIONS

Enough isn't just about closets and cupboards. It applies to our schedules, our work, even our ambition.

Time.

In a culture that glorifies busyness, many of us overfill our calendars. Enough time doesn't mean idleness; it means space for what matters most — dinners with family, mornings of reflection, weekends for rest.

Work.

Success is often measured by promotions and bigger paychecks. But enough in work may mean stability, balance, or meaningful contribution — not endless ascent.

Ambition.

Dreaming big is human, but unbounded ambition robs us of peace. Enough is knowing when to stop chasing and start savoring. These shifts in perspective replace quantity with clarity. Instead of asking How much more can I do? we begin to ask What deserves my energy?

While possessions, time, work, and ambition are powerful categories, it can also help to explore specific domains of life where "enough" can be practiced:

Money.

Financial security is essential, but beyond a certain point, research shows extra income adds little happiness. Enough money means stability and freedom from constant worry — not limitless accumulation.

Food.

In a culture of oversized portions, enough food means nourishment and enjoyment without excess. Eating until satisfied, rather than stuffed, is a practice in gratitude and restraint.

Digital Life.

Many of us are drowning in information. Enough might mean fewer apps, fewer notifications, or one hour of intentional scrolling rather than four of mindless consumption.

Relationships.

Not every connection needs to be deep. Enough relationships means investing in the ones that nourish us and releasing the ones that drain us.

Thinking of enough in these domains grounds the concept in everyday choices. It shifts the abstract into the tangible: how we spend, eat, connect, and click. Each is an invitation to practice sufficiency.

THE ABUNDANCE OF ENOUGH

When we release the pressure to add, we often discover we already have more than we realized. Fewer possessions bring peace. Homes and minds feel calmer without overflow. Reclaimed time brings presence. Moments with loved ones feel richer. Letting go of endless striving brings gratitude. We savor what's already here. Defining sufficiency brings clarity. Decisions become simpler, boundaries stronger. This kind of abundance is quieter than achievement or acquisition, but far more enduring.

PROTECTING ENOUGH

The world won't stop selling "more" just because we've chosen sufficiency. Protecting enough takes intention.

Pause.

Before buying or committing, ask: Does this serve my definition of enough?

Limit input.

Reduce exposure to ads and feeds that stir comparison.

Practice gratitude.

Begin or end each day noticing what's already good.

Choose simplicity.

Rotate the clothes you love, cook with fewer tools,

block off time for rest.

Find community.

Surround yourself with people who value presence over possessions.

Most of all, remember: enough is a practice, not a destination. Some days it feels natural; other days, fragile. What matters is returning again and again to your own definition.

THE QUIET POWER

The power of enough lies in its quiet clarity. It doesn't dazzle or shout. It whispers — but in that whisper is a freedom louder than anything "more" could offer.

Enough allows us to stop comparing, stop cluttering, stop striving endlessly. It helps us savor what we already have. It restores balance in a world of extremes. And it sustains us, because while "more" always demands more, enough requires only gratitude and care.

Enough doesn't mean scarcity. It means fullness

without excess, peace without burden, and joy without striving. Choosing enough is not resignation. It is empowerment.

And once we know the power of enough, the natural next step is clear: to shape our lives around it. In the following chapter, we'll explore living with less — not as punishment, but as a way of creating more space for joy, clarity, and meaning.

Defining enough doesn't just transform individual lives — it reshapes communities and even the planet. A culture built on endless consumption strains natural resources and widens inequality. By contrast, people who embrace sufficiency tend to waste less, share more, and focus on contribution instead of competition.

On a personal level, enough nurtures generosity. When we no longer chase accumulation, we have more time and energy to give — to relationships, creativity, and causes that matter. On a societal level, movements like voluntary simplicity or minimalism show that redefining success in terms of sufficiency rather than excess can ripple outward. Imagine workplaces where balance is prized over burnout, or neighborhoods where connection matters more than square footage.

Even our legacy shifts. More is rarely remembered. But living with enough — and modeling gratitude, balance, and generosity — leaves behind something enduring: a life that showed others there is another way.

Enough, then, is not just a private choice. It's a contribution to a healthier, more humane world.

CHAPTER SIX
LIVING WITH LESS

If the power of enough is a mindset, then living with less is the practice that makes it real. It is the movement from idea to embodiment, from philosophy to habit. Living with less is not about deprivation or austerity. It is a conscious decision to create space for what matters by gently setting aside what doesn't.

The word less often carries shadows. We've been

trained to hear it as loss: less money, less comfort, less opportunity. But in truth, less can be liberation. Less distraction means more focus. Fewer possessions mean fewer demands on our time. What looks like subtraction is actually addition, because every "less" makes room for a greater "more": more peace, more joy, more presence.

BEGINNING SMALL

Living with less rarely begins with sweeping gestures. You don't need to empty your home in a weekend or haul half your belongings to the curb. It often begins with a single drawer or a single decision — releasing one item you don't use, saying no to one commitment you don't need. These small acts create relief, and together they build momentum.

The beauty is that this practice looks different for everyone. For one person, it may mean simplifying a wardrobe to only clothes that fit and feel good. For another, it might mean trimming digital clutter — fewer apps, fewer notifications, fewer hours lost to scrolling. For someone else, it could mean downsizing to a smaller home in order to trade upkeep for time and flexibility. There is no single formula. Living with less is not about following rules, but about aligning life with values.

WHY LETTING GO FEELS HARD

Objects are rarely just objects. They carry stories, memories, and fragments of identity. A sweater might symbolize a friendship. A gadget might embody a dream of being more creative. A set of dishes might hold the memory of family dinners long past. That's why letting go can feel like betrayal.

Psychologists call this the endowment effect — our tendency to overvalue what we own simply because it's ours. One study showed that people asked to sell a mug they'd just been given demanded nearly twice as much as they themselves had been willing to pay for it. Ownership tricks the brain into believing an object is more necessary than it really is.

Recognizing this bias makes the process easier. Neuroscientists studying habits note that our brains run on routines to conserve energy. The basal ganglia, a region involved in habit formation, automates repeated actions — from brushing our teeth to where we place our keys. Unfortunately, clutter itself can become a habit: buying without thinking, keeping without questioning. Breaking the cycle requires intentional interruption. Behavioral researchers suggest small "keystone habits" — like making the bed each morning or clearing the kitchen counter every night — which set off a cascade of order. Once a new habit of simplicity is established, it reinforces itself, making future choices to live with less feel natural rather than forced. When you realize the pull is psychological, not practical, the grip loosens. You can honor the memory without holding onto the material. You can release the gadget without discarding the creativity it once represented. You can let go and discover that life not only continues — it feels lighter.

A friend once told me about cleaning out her grandmother's attic after she passed away. At first, the family felt overwhelmed by the sheer volume of boxes stacked to the ceiling — decades of clothes, trinkets, and keepsakes. But as they worked, they noticed something striking: the objects their grandmother had treasured most weren't hidden in those boxes at all. They were the photographs worn from handling, the recipe cards stained with use, the quilt patched again and again because it had been loved into fraying. The rest — piles of magazines, unopened gifts, gadgets long out of use — had only gathered dust. "It made me realize," my friend said, "that what we hold onto isn't always what holds value." That moment reshaped the way she thought about her own possessions. She began asking herself: Will this matter in thirty years? Will someone else see the meaning, or will they only see a box to sort through?

THE REWARDS OF SPACE

When less becomes practice, the rewards arrive quickly. Walk into a decluttered room and you feel it — the quiet of open space. Look at a pared-back calendar and you see it — evenings free for rest or connection. Instead of chasing life, you begin living it.

Research backs this up. Studies show the average adult makes around 35,000 decisions per day. Every unnecessary option — which shirt to wear, which app to open, which stack of papers to sort —

eats into limited mental energy. Psychologists call this "decision fatigue." Living with less reduces the number of small, draining choices, leaving more energy for the decisions that actually matter. A 2016 UCLA study on families and clutter found that mothers who described their homes as "cluttered" showed significantly higher cortisol levels throughout the day. Conversely, participants who simplified their environments reported lower stress and greater well-being. Less isn't just emotional; it's physiological.

And simplicity doesn't only clear shelves; it reshapes the rhythm of daily life. Mornings are calmer when closets hold only clothes you actually wear. Kitchens become joyful places when only the tools you love remain. A desk stripped of paper piles doesn't stifle creativity — it invites it. When the background noise of excess quiets, the signal of what you value grows stronger.

FREEDOM, CREATIVITY AND JOY

The paradox of less is that it doesn't restrict — it expands.

Creativity flourishes when the noise fades. Psychologists at the University of Minnesota found that tidy environments promote healthier choices and greater focus, while open, uncluttered spaces are linked with innovative thinking. A child surrounded by fewer toys often invents more imaginative games. Adults, too, find their creativity unlocked when their environment stops demanding constant attention.

Freedom grows when we are no longer tethered to maintenance. Every item we own requires something from us — storage, cleaning, repair, or eventual disposal. Fewer possessions mean fewer obligations. A smaller home may mean fewer expenses and more mobility. Fewer gadgets mean fewer cords, updates, and frustrations. What looks like restriction is actually flexibility: life becomes more mobile, open, and responsive.

Joy deepens when we shift from acquisition to presence. Researchers at Harvard found that people who spend money to "buy time" — outsourcing chores, reducing errands — report greater life satisfaction than those who spend on goods. By living with less, we reclaim hours once lost to cleaning, shopping, or organizing. Paradoxically, fewer possessions don't just create space on our shelves; they expand our sense of time itself. Instead of being distracted by guilt over unused equipment or endless to-do lists, we notice more — the way sunlight falls across the floor, the laughter at a family dinner, the taste of coffee at a clear table. These are not extraordinary experiences; they are ordinary ones, finally visible because the noise has receded.

The benefits of living with less are not only emotional but financial. Studies show the average American household spends over $1,700 annually on nonessential items — purchases later admitted to be unnecessary. Add in storage costs (a $40-billion-a-year industry in the U.S.), and the price of excess climbs even higher. By contrast, households that intentionally simplify often report lower monthly expenses, faster debt repayment, and greater savings for experiences like travel or education. Living with less isn't about denial; it's about redirecting resources away from clutter and toward meaning.

FAMILIES AND COMMUNITIES

Living with less doesn't just transform individuals — it reshapes families and communities.

Within households, possessions are often silent sources of tension. Parents argue over purchases. Couples clash about clutter. Children squabble over toys. But when a family commits to less, something shifts. Decisions become easier, rooms feel calmer, and conversations move from What should we buy? to What should we do together?

I once spoke with a family who sold their large house, moved into a smaller one, and donated much of what they had accumulated. At first, they worried their children would feel deprived. Instead, the opposite happened. With fewer toys, play became more imaginative. With fewer distractions, the family spent more time outdoors, cooking together, playing board games. "We thought we were giving something up," the parents said, "but what we actually gained was family."

The same pattern extends to neighborhoods. When possessions stop being measures of status, communities rediscover sharing. Instead of every household owning a ladder, neighbors borrow. Instead of stockpiling gadgets, communities create tool libraries. Instead of endless piles of forgotten toys, families trade and donate. These choices reduce waste but also rebuild trust. Living with less has an environmental echo as well. The average American throws away over 80 pounds of clothing each year, and millions of tons of furniture end up in landfills annually. Choosing to buy less, reuse longer, and share within communities doesn't just lighten households — it lightens the planet's load. Minimalist households often discover that by consuming less, they reduce their carbon footprint and align their daily choices with the larger goal of sustainability.

And even celebrations take on new depth. Holidays and birthdays, once buried under piles of gifts, feel lighter when they center on experiences. Families who replace stacks of presents with shared meals, storytelling, or outings often describe those memories as more lasting than anything wrapped in paper.

Mental health researchers are beginning to document the psychological effects of simplicity. A

2019 survey published in the Journal of Positive Psychology found that people who described themselves as practicing "voluntary simplicity" reported higher levels of life satisfaction and lower levels of anxiety compared to peers. Another study linked decluttering with improved sleep quality, suggesting that orderly spaces help the nervous system regulate at night. When families and communities embrace less, the gains extend beyond cleaner homes — they include calmer minds, healthier bodies, and stronger connections.

A PRACTICE NOT A PROJECT

Living with less isn't a one-time purge. It's an ongoing practice — a daily conversation with ourselves. Each day brings new questions: What do I need? What can I release? What truly brings me life? The answers shift over time because we change. What felt essential five years ago may not serve us today.

Small tools help along the way. A "maybe box" allows us to set aside items we're unsure about, checking later if we missed them. Daily or weekly goals — one item released, one drawer cleared — keep progress steady without overwhelm. Most importantly, reframing release as generosity transforms the process. One powerful habit is a "weekly reset." Choose a set time — Sunday evening, Friday afternoon — to scan your home and schedule. Put away what has drifted out of place, clear surfaces, cancel or reschedule commitments that no longer serve you. This ritual keeps simplicity alive, preventing clutter and obligations from quietly creeping back in. Over time, it becomes less about tidying and more about aligning life with intention. When we donate something, it doesn't vanish; it goes to someone who may need it more. Letting go becomes an act of abundance.

To make living with less more tangible, try weaving in small practices:

The One-In, One-Out Rule: *For every new item that enters your home, one leaves. This keeps possessions at equilibrium.*

The 10-Minute Sweep: *Set a timer and reset one area of your home daily. It's enough to build* *momentum without overwhelm.*

Experience Audit: *Once a month, review your calendar. Highlight the activities that gave you energy, and cross out those that drained you. Use this to guide future commitments.*

The Gratitude Shelf: *Choose one shelf or surface in your home to display only what you truly cherish — a photo, a memento, a book. Let it remind you that value is not in quantity but in meaning.*

THE ABUNDANCE BENEATH THE NOISE

One of the most surprising discoveries about living with less is that it doesn't feel like sacrifice. Quite the opposite: it feels like expansion. Less clutter, less debt, less stress. More space, more energy, more calm. The math of simplicity is paradoxical: subtraction leads to multiplication.

And in the space left behind, gratitude naturally grows. Once the noise of excess is quieted, the ordinary begins to shine — the warmth of morning sunlight, the sound of laughter, the small details of daily life. Gratitude fills the space we've created. It shifts the spotlight from scarcity to sufficiency, from what's missing to what remains.

In a culture that profits from our dissatisfaction, living with less can even be seen as an act of quiet resistance. Every time you choose not to buy, you are rejecting the story that happiness is for sale. Every time you pause before clicking "add to cart," you reclaim authorship of your own contentment. These choices may seem small, but they accumulate into a life that says no to being defined by consumption and yes to being defined by presence.

Living with less is not about stripping life bare. It is about removing what gets in the way so that what matters most can breathe. It is not about deprivation, but liberation. And when paired with gratitude, it becomes a way of life that feels not smaller, but infinitely larger.

A SIMPLE PRACTICE

Before you move on, pause for just five minutes. Look around the room you're in and choose one thing you no longer need. Set it aside — tomorrow you can donate, recycle, or simply release it. Then, notice one thing you already have that brings you comfort or joy. Sit with that feeling for a moment. This pairing — letting go of the unnecessary while savoring what remains — is the quiet rhythm of living with less. Each time you repeat it, you step more fully into a life that feels lighter, calmer, and more your own.

CHAPTER SEVEN
THE QUIET POWER OF GRATITUDE

If living with less clears space in our lives, gratitude is what fills it with meaning. Gratitude is more than saying "thank you." It is a way of seeing, a lens that turns our focus from what's missing to what's present. It teaches us to notice the ordinary—and find the extraordinary within it.

The power of gratitude lies in its simplicity. We often imagine happiness as something to chase, but gratitude reveals it as something already here. A cup of coffee in the morning, the sound of rain on the roof, the smile of a stranger — these details are easy to miss in the rush of daily life. Gratitude slows us long enough to notice them, and in noticing, transforms them into gifts.

What makes gratitude potent is not that it changes circumstances, but that it changes how we perceive them. A cluttered home can feel oppressive until we recognize the comfort it provides. A modest paycheck can feel insufficient until we remember it still puts food on the table and a roof overhead. Gratitude doesn't deny challenges; it reframes them by highlighting what remains steady, supportive, and good.

Modern research backs this up. People who practice gratitude regularly report higher well-being, stronger relationships, and better physical health. Gratitude journaling has been linked to reduced stress and improved sleep. But beyond studies, gratitude works because it trains our attention. We find what we look for: search for scarcity and you'll feel it everywhere; look for sufficiency and abundance appears in unexpected places.

Gratitude also disrupts the myth of more. Consumer culture thrives on dissatisfaction; gratitude interrupts it by reminding us that what we already have is enough. When we pause to appreciate the shoes on our feet, the roof overhead, or the meal on the table, we loosen the pull of constant craving. Life stops feeling like a deficit to fix and starts looking like a gift to enjoy.

This shift doesn't require dramatic change. You don't need to abandon your job or move to the countryside. It can begin with something as small as naming three things you're thankful for at the end of the day. Over time, these acknowledgments accumulate, reshaping how you experience life. Gratitude becomes less of an exercise and more of a reflex — a natural way of seeing.

In a noisy world that demands more, gratitude offers quiet resistance. It says: I see what is here. I value it. It is enough. And in that simple recognition, we discover the contentment we've been searching for — not on the horizon, but in the very moment we are living now.

Gratitude sounds effortless in theory; in practice, it requires intention. It's easy to feel thankful when life is smooth, harder when bills loom or uncertainty shadows the day. That is why gratitude must be understood not just as a feeling, but as a discipline — a deliberate act of shifting perspective.

Think of it as training. Just as muscles grow through repeated use, gratitude strengthens through repeated attention. At first, it may feel awkward or forced. Writing down a few things you're grateful for might seem small compared to the weight of real problems. But with consistency, the practice changes the way you notice the world. Gratitude isn't about ignoring difficulties; it's about refusing to let them obscure everything else.

Consider someone recovering from illness. Gratitude in that season might not be for perfect health, but for the meal a friend delivered, the doctor who listened carefully, or the moment of energy that allowed a walk outside. These acknowledgments don't erase hardship, but they soften its edge. They remind us that even in struggle, life still contains goodness worth noticing.

Reframing works the same way. Instead of asking, Why is this happening to me? gratitude asks, What can I learn here? What is still steady right now? For someone who loses a job, this might mean appreciating the chance to rest, or noticing the support of loved ones, or recognizing the possibility of a new path forward. Gratitude doesn't deny the loss — it simply refuses to let loss define the entire story.

Our minds naturally gravitate toward gaps and imperfections. Advertising amplifies this by pointing out what we lack. Gratitude is counter-training. It says: look again — at what's here, working, sustaining, supporting. It is a deliberate redirection of focus.

Simple practices anchor this shift. Keep a short gratitude journal. Make it social by telling a friend, partner, or colleague something specific you appreciate about them. Pause before a meal to acknowledge the hands and resources that brought it to the table. These acts train perception.

THE SCIENCE OF GRATITUDE

Neuroscience offers a fascinating glimpse into why gratitude feels so transformative. Brain imaging studies show that when we practice gratitude — whether by journaling, writing a letter, or simply pausing to reflect — regions of the brain linked to reward, empathy, and decision-making become more active. The prefrontal cortex, associated with planning and perspective, lights up. The anterior cingulate cortex, which helps regulate emotions, shows increased activity. Even the brain's dopamine pathways — the same circuits activated by pleasurable experiences — respond to gratitude. In other words, gratitude literally reshapes the brain to notice and savor positive experiences more readily.

Researchers at Indiana University found that people who engaged in structured gratitude exercises continued to show stronger brain responses to generosity months later. Gratitude didn't just create a temporary mood boost; it rewired their perception of life. This explains why consistent practice matters. A single moment of thankfulness may feel good, but repeated attention builds lasting patterns. Gratitude, in this sense, is not only an attitude but a form of mental training — a quiet way of strengthening resilience at the neurological level.

What begins as discipline becomes habit. Over time, gratitude reshapes the lens through which we interpret life. It doesn't erase difficulty, but it ensures difficulty never eclipses everything else.

Gratitude steadies us, grounding us in sufficiency even when circumstances feel fragile.

GRATITUDE ACROSS CULTURES

Though modern science affirms gratitude's benefits, the practice itself is ancient and universal. Many Indigenous cultures center communal gratitude rituals, offering thanks not just for food or shelter but for the land, the seasons, and the interconnectedness of life. In Japan, the word arigatou literally means "difficult to exist," a reminder that every kindness, no matter how small, is a gift not to be taken for granted. In parts of Africa, communal meals often begin with spoken thanks not only to ancestors but to the farmers, cooks, and community members whose efforts made the gathering possible.

Religious traditions echo this theme. In Christianity, prayers of thanksgiving are woven into daily practice. In Buddhism, gratitude is expressed for the interdependence of all beings. In Hindu rituals, offerings are given in recognition of life's sustaining forces. Despite cultural differences, the core pattern is the same: gratitude ties us to something larger than ourselves.

This universality reminds us that gratitude is not a modern self-help technique but a timeless human practice. It has always been a way of resisting isolation, of seeing sufficiency where scarcity might otherwise dominate, of remembering that life itself is a gift. When we engage in gratitude today — whether through journaling, prayer, or pausing to notice sunlight on the floor — we are joining a lineage of people across centuries and cultures who have practiced the same act of noticing and giving thanks.

The quiet power of gratitude becomes clearest when we see it lived out. Sometimes it appears in ordinary moments, other times in extraordinary ones. What unites them is not the scale of circumstance but the shift in perspective.

I once met a teacher working in a school with few resources. The classrooms were crowded, supplies scarce, challenges constant. Yet she radiated joy. When I asked how she stayed positive, she said, "Every day I'm grateful for the kids' laughter. They remind me why I'm here." Her gratitude wasn't for perfect conditions but for small, steady signs of life.

Another story comes from a man who lost nearly

everything in a house fire — his home, possessions, years of memories. In the days after, when grief could have overwhelmed him, what he spoke about instead was gratitude. "The fire took a lot," he said, "but it didn't take my family. That's what matters." His gratitude gave him a foundation to stand on.

Gratitude also shows up in quieter ways. A young couple I once visited lived in a tiny apartment with secondhand furniture and a view of the alley. By most standards, their life looked modest. Yet they described themselves as happy. They cooked together, laughed often, and dreamed freely. "We make a point to notice what we already have," the husband told me. "A warm home. Food on the table. Each other. That's enough."

And then there was a retiree who practiced gratitude as ritual. Each morning she walked her garden, naming things she appreciated aloud: the way the light hit the leaves, the sound of birds, the rhythm of her breath. "It keeps me from rushing," she said. "I start the day by remembering it's already good."

These examples reveal something essential: gratitude isn't about circumstances. It's about attention. The crowded classroom didn't change.

The fire victim's loss didn't vanish. The couple's apartment didn't expand. The garden didn't bloom forever. What changed was the lens through which they chose to see. Gratitude didn't erase hardship, but it reframed it, allowing joy to coexist alongside difficulty.

These stories remind us that gratitude is available to anyone, anywhere. We don't need perfect conditions to practice it. We only need the willingness to pause and notice what is good.

Gratitude doesn't just change how we see life; it changes how we see each other. Viewed through appreciation, relationships soften. Resentment eases. Bonds deepen. Expressed, gratitude becomes one of the simplest — and most powerful — forces in human connection.

Think of how often we notice what others lack. A spouse forgets a chore, a colleague misses a detail, a friend cancels plans. Left unchecked, these moments accumulate into frustration. But when we focus on what they contribute — the chore completed, the effort made, the friend's presence in harder times — the balance changes. Gratitude doesn't excuse mistakes, but it prevents them from defining the relationship.

Spoken aloud, gratitude transforms further. A simple "I appreciate you for..." strengthens trust and intimacy. Couples who regularly express gratitude report higher satisfaction. Friendships deepen when thanks is shared openly. Even workplace teams thrive when appreciation is part of the culture. Gratitude is contagious — when we hear it, we want to pass it on.

It also heals comparison. In a consumer-driven world, it's easy to measure relationships by status: who has the bigger house, the better job, the flashier vacation. Comparison breeds envy, and envy corrodes connection. Gratitude interrupts this cycle. When we are thankful for people as they are — not as society measures them — envy loses its grip. A friend's success becomes something to celebrate, not compete against.

Gratitude also carries humility. Saying "thank you" acknowledges that we need others, that we cannot do everything alone. This vulnerability fosters trust. It reminds people they matter, not just for what they do but for who they are. Gratitude affirms dignity.

Even in conflict, gratitude can be a bridge. A heated argument shifts when one person pauses to say, "I'm frustrated, but I'm also grateful that you care enough to have this conversation." Such acknowledgments don't erase disagreement, but they soften its edges.

Families especially benefit. Children who practice gratitude — not just as manners, but as mindfulness — often grow up more resilient and empathetic. Parents who model it create homes where appreciation is the norm, not the exception. These households may not have more possessions, but they often have more joy.

At its heart, gratitude in relationships is about attention. When we notice and name the good in others, we draw it closer. We stop taking people for granted and start seeing them clearly. And when we see clearly, connection flourishes.

While gratitude often begins outward — noticing kindness, beauty, or comfort — its deepest work happens inward. It softens the harsh ways we speak to ourselves and replaces inadequacy with worthiness.

Many of us carry an inner script of not enough. Not smart enough. Not successful enough. Not attractive enough. These messages, reinforced by advertising and comparison, shape how we see ourselves: perpetually lacking, always behind. Gratitude interrupts that script. It asks us to notice what is already present within us.

Consider the difference between these thoughts: "I didn't accomplish everything I planned today" versus "I'm grateful for the progress I made." The first highlights deficiency; the second highlights sufficiency. Gratitude doesn't ignore growth, but it frames it with appreciation.

Self-directed gratitude can feel unfamiliar. Many people are more comfortable offering kindness to others than themselves. But cultivating it inwardly is vital. It builds resilience. It reminds us that even on hard days, we are more capable and resourceful than we admit.

Practical exercises help. At the end of the day, instead of writing only external gratitudes, note three things about yourself you appreciate: patience in a tough conversation, effort on a project, courage to rest when needed. Over time, these acknowledgments form a record of sufficiency that counters the relentless story of not enough.

Gratitude also deepens self-acceptance. When we are grateful for our bodies — not for how they look, but for how they carry us — we stop measuring them only by appearance. When we are grateful for our talents — even if they seem small or ordinary — we stop comparing them to others. Gratitude shifts our inner gaze from critique to appreciation, and appreciation nurtures peace.

This doesn't mean denying weakness. It means holding it alongside strength. It means seeing that even in imperfection, we carry gifts worth valuing. Gratitude teaches us to view ourselves not as projects to fix but as beings to cherish.

As we practice gratitude toward ourselves, we become more authentic with others. When we no longer feel defined by lack, we no longer need to prove our worth through possessions or appearances. Gratitude grounds identity in presence, not performance. We begin to live from sufficiency, carrying the quiet assurance: I am enough.

When practiced daily, gratitude becomes more than a mood or a moment — it becomes a way of inhabiting the world. It reshapes our inner dialogue, our relationships, our work, and the ordinary fabric of life.

The first shift is presence. Gratitude requires slowing down. You can't notice sunlight on your face while scrolling distractions. You can't savor a meal if you're already planning the next task. Gratitude anchors us in the now, asking us to see what is here before rushing toward what's next.

The second shift is perspective. Gratitude trains the mind to see sufficiency instead of scarcity. Over time, this becomes reflexive. Where once you looked at a modest paycheck and saw lack, now you see provision. Where once you saw a small home as limitation, now you see shelter and comfort. Gratitude doesn't blind us to difficulty, but it prevents difficulty from eclipsing everything else.

The third shift is resilience. Life inevitably brings hardship — illness, loss, uncertainty, change. Gratitude doesn't remove pain, but it helps us endure it. By noticing what still remains, what still sustains, we find strength to continue.

Gratitude also expands generosity. Recognizing abundance makes us less inclined to cling and more free to share. Gratitude dissolves envy and nurtures empathy. It softens judgment, replacing it with appreciation for the diverse ways people contribute to the whole.

Even at work, gratitude changes the atmosphere. Teams that practice appreciation experience less burnout and more collaboration. Leaders who express gratitude foster loyalty. Employees who celebrate small wins sustain morale. In creative fields, gratitude fuels innovation by shifting focus from fear of failure to appreciation for opportunity.

Most importantly, gratitude creates joy out of the ordinary. The commute becomes a chance to listen to music or reflect. Washing dishes becomes a moment to appreciate the meal just shared. The rhythm of waking and sleeping becomes a reminder that life itself is a gift. Gratitude doesn't wait for extraordinary circumstances — it elevates the everyday.

This is why gratitude, though quiet, is powerful. It doesn't need fanfare. It transforms by accumulation — the steady layering of noticed, appreciated moments. Over time, these moments form a foundation of contentment no amount of "more" could replicate.

Living with less opens the door. Gratitude teaches us how to walk through it and make a home there. Together, they create a life marked not by striving, but by sufficiency — not by craving, but by peace.

Gratitude is quiet, but its effects reverberate. It

softens scarcity, calms the restless chase for more, and restores attention to what is already good. In a culture that measures life by accumulation, gratitude is an act of resistance. It says: I do not need more to be whole. I already have enough.

This doesn't mean life becomes perfect. Gratitude doesn't erase hardship. Bills still arrive. Relationships face conflict. Challenges still disrupt plans. What gratitude offers is not immunity from difficulty, but resilience within it. It reminds us that even in the darkest seasons, some light remains — a friend's encouragement, a warm meal, the simple fact of breath in our lungs.

What makes gratitude transformative is its accessibility. You don't need wealth or training to practice it. You don't need to wait for conditions to improve. Gratitude begins wherever you are, with whatever you already have. It is found in the smallest details: a sip of water, a note of music, a shared smile.

This practice isn't about ignoring ambition. Ambition and gratitude are not enemies. Ambition looks forward; gratitude looks around. Together they balance us — ambition propels, gratitude steadies. Without ambition, we stagnate. Without gratitude, we never feel satisfied.

As this chapter closes, one truth becomes clear: gratitude isn't something to practice only when life is smooth. It is especially powerful when life is not. By choosing to notice and appreciate what remains, we cultivate a strength that outlasts possessions, achievements, or recognition. Gratitude becomes the anchor that holds amid change.

And as gratitude steadies us, it prepares us for the next challenge: comparison. Even with gratitude, the world whispers that others have more — more success, more beauty, more status, more comfort. That whisper is comparison, and it can unravel appreciation if left unchecked.

Next, we'll name that trap, see how it steals joy, and learn how to replace it with something more life-giving — so gratitude has room to last. Gratitude shows us life is already rich. Escaping comparison ensures we don't lose sight of that richness by looking over someone else's shoulder. Together, they lead us toward a life not only simpler, but freer.

CHAPTER EIGHT
ESCAPING THE COMPARISON TRAP

Even the most grateful heart can wobble with a single glance sideways. You may feel perfectly at ease in your own home until a neighbor's renovation gleams next door. You can feel proud of your work until a colleague receives the promotion you hoped for. You may love your vacation until a scroll reveals someone else's tropical escape. Comparison is subtle, but it is powerful—and, left unchecked, it unravels peace with alarming speed.

The impulse itself is ancient. Human beings have always looked side to side, gauging where they stood in the tribe. Once, this instinct kept us alive. Knowing who was stronger, who held resources, who carried influence—these once meant safety. But in the modern world, that reflex often works against us. Instead of protecting, it unsettles. Instead of bonding, it isolates. We measure our lives against curated images, inflated titles, and highlight reels that conceal the struggle behind them. And each time we seem to come up short—often only in perception—contentment thins.

Nowhere is this dynamic more amplified than on social media. With a flick of the thumb, we are immersed in hundreds of lives, each presented as brighter, easier, richer, more enviable than our own. We know, at least in theory, these are curated—filtered, polished, sometimes exaggerated.

Research confirms what our emotions already reveal. A 2018 study published in Journal of Social and Clinical Psychology found that reducing social media use to just 30 minutes per day led to significant decreases in loneliness and depression. Another large survey by the American Psychological

Association reported that nearly 60% of adults say social media creates feelings of inadequacy about their own lives. Among young adults, the numbers climb higher, with over 70% admitting that scrolling often leaves them less satisfied with their circumstances. These aren't abstract findings — they are the measurable cost of constant comparison.

Yet intellect is powerless against emotion. We still feel the sting. What once felt like enough begins to feel inadequate. Gratitude falters, envy flourishes, and peace erodes in the endless scroll. I remember speaking with a college student who described this vividly. She had worked all summer to save for a short road trip with friends — a modest adventure, camping along the coast. She was proud of it until she logged onto Instagram. Her feed was filled with classmates posting from Europe, from luxury resorts, from concerts in far-off cities. What had felt like freedom just hours earlier suddenly seemed embarrassing. "It was like my trip shrank," she said. Nothing about her experience had changed — the laughter in the car, the beauty of the shoreline, the sense of independence. But the comparison reframed it as "less than." That is the trap in action: joy quietly eroded by someone else's highlight reel.

But comparison doesn't live only on screens. It shows up in familiar rooms: at family gatherings, where siblings' milestones are weighed in unspoken rankings; in offices, where recognition, raises, and opportunities feel uneven; in friendships, where engagements, promotions, or children become silent scoreboards; in neighborhoods, where lawns, cars, or vacations are measured without words. The trap is everywhere, tugging us off sufficiency and into scarcity.

The first step toward freedom is recognizing its cost. Constant comparison drains us. It blurs the texture of our own lives. We stop noticing what is good, unique, and meaningful about our journey. We dismiss our milestones because they don't match someone else's timeline. We trade joy for insecurity, peace for envy. And the cruel truth is this: comparison has no finish line. There will always be someone with more—another ladder, another rung, another race that cannot be won.

The alternative is not isolation or withdrawal. We are not asked to stop noticing others. The invitation is to shift the frame. Instead of asking, How do I compare? we ask, Am I aligned with what matters to me? Instead of borrowing someone else's yardstick, we carve our own from what matters. That subtle shift frees us from the endless ladder and sets us again on the steady ground of sufficiency.

Escaping comparison doesn't mean envy never arises. It will. The whispers won't vanish; they're human nature. Freedom lies in noticing when envy speaks and choosing not to obey. It lies in replacing the reflex to measure with the practice of appreciation—both for ourselves and for others. Your life was never meant to be theirs. It was always meant to be yours.

IDENTITY WITHOUT THE SCOREBOARD

Comparison doesn't only shrink joy in the moment—it erodes identity over time. You complete something meaningful—a degree, a promotion, a creative milestone—and feel proud. Then you see someone who went "further": a more prestigious school, a bigger title, louder recognition. Your achievement hasn't changed, but your perception has. Comparison downsizes what once brought joy.

This cycle never ends. If your worth hinges on staying ahead, satisfaction will always be delayed. The race has no tape to break.

Freedom requires a shift from relative worth to inherent worth. Not How do I measure up? but Who am I apart from measurement? That doesn't cancel ambition; it relocates identity. It grounds us not in outcomes but in values.

Practical moves help:

1. Define your markers.

Choose measures of a good life that fit you: meaningful work, time with family, creative practice, health, service, spiritual depth. If you're aligned with these, you're succeeding—regardless of anyone else's results.

2. Name your contributions.

List qualities and skills that make you you. Note how they show up at home, at work, in community. Another's success never erased these; it never will.

3. Curate your inputs.

If certain feeds, rooms, or conversations consistently leave you "less than," adjust your exposure. Guarding identity isn't avoidance; it's wisdom.

Over time, worth feels less like a fluctuating stock and more like something steady—rooted in being, not benchmarking.

GRATITUDE AS THE ANTIDOTE

Where comparison whispers, Look at what they have that you don't, gratitude counters, Look at what you have that matters. The two cannot coexist for long. Comparison fuels envy; gratitude fuels contentment.

This is why gratitude is more than a warm feeling—it is a deliberate strategy. It pulls attention inward, toward what is already present. It doesn't erase ambition; it grounds it. From sufficiency, you can still pursue growth—without the panic of keeping up.

Gratitude also widens our capacity to celebrate others. Thankful people are harder to threaten by others' wins. A friend's promotion becomes joy rather than a jab. A neighbor's upgrade becomes interesting rather than indicting. You can say,

"Good for them," without the hidden, "Why not me?"

Practice helps:

1. Pair comparison with thanks.

When envy flares—during a scroll or an announcement—pause and name three things in your life you are glad for. Their win can remain theirs; your peace remains yours.

2. Voice appreciation.

Tell someone, "I'm happy for you," and mean it. Spoken gratitude turns rivalry into relationship.

3. Anchor before you aim.

Let gratitude set the baseline: I am enough. From there, goals become chosen paths, not proofs of worth.

Gratitude brings humility, too. Much of what we enjoy—opportunities, mentorship, timing—is grace. Seeing that makes room to honor the grace in others' stories as well.

PRACTICAL GUARDRAILS

Mindset matters, but so do habits. We need supports that keep us off comparison's treadmill:

1. Redefine success

If success equals a number, an image, or a title, comparison will own you. Define success as alignment with your values. Different values, different race.

2. Curate your environment

Unfollow accounts that agitate inadequacy. Limit spaces where status is the main sport. Seek inputs that affirm sufficiency and substance.

3. Make appreciation a ritual

A short nightly gratitude list, a family "one good thing" at dinner, a weekly walk naming small blessings—rituals retrain attention.

4. Celebrate progress

Comparison fixates on endpoints; life is lived in steps. Mark the step: the draft finished, the run attempted, the brave conversation had.

5. Trade envy for curiosity

Ask, What can I learn from their path? Borrow the

principle without adopting the pressure.

6. Practice presence

Most comparing happens when we're not where we are. Return to your work, your people, your breath. In the present, the scoreboard fades.

These guardrails won't mute every whisper, but they shorten their half-life. They help us recognize comparison for what it is and return more quickly to what matters.

STORIES THAT SHOW THE TRAP

Consider a workplace where recognition is unevenly distributed. One person's contributions are publicly celebrated while others, equally diligent, go unnoticed. For the overlooked, comparison becomes almost unavoidable. Their sense of worth diminishes not because their work is less valuable, but because it was measured against a colleague's moment in the spotlight. Left unchecked, such moments can erode morale—not just for individuals but for entire teams.

Or take the family gathering where siblings' achievements are lined up—houses bought, careers advanced, children raised. Rarely does anyone say outright, "Who's ahead?" Yet the unspoken math is palpable. Those who feel "behind" leave the table quieter, carrying the invisible burden of inadequacy. In reality, each life unfolds on its own timetable, shaped by circumstances often hidden from view. Still, comparison tempts us to flatten those differences into a single hierarchy.

Creative fields provide another lens. An artist may complete a painting that once felt inspired—until scrolling reveals another's work that garners thousands of likes. Suddenly, what was fulfilling becomes inferior. Comparison not only robs satisfaction but can stifle expression altogether, as the artist begins to create not from passion but from pressure to compete.

What unites these examples is not failure of character but vulnerability of perspective. Our instinct to measure is natural. The danger lies in allowing those measurements to become the story we tell ourselves about our worth.

THE PSYCHOLOGY BEHIND IT

Researchers describe two kinds of comparison: upward and downward. Upward comparison looks at those "ahead" of us. It can inspire growth but, when laced with envy, breeds discouragement. Downward comparison looks at those "behind" us. It can produce gratitude, but it can also tempt arrogance. Both distort the truth. Both distract from living our own story.

Psychologists call this cycle social comparison theory and note how relentless exposure— especially through media—amplifies dissatisfaction. When we see hundreds of lives daily, curated and condensed, we engage in upward comparison far more than downward. We are perpetually reminded of what we lack, seldom of what we already hold. The result is a chronic sense of scarcity, even when our circumstances are objectively sufficient.

The irony is that comparison rarely reveals reality. The colleague who seems effortlessly successful may be privately struggling. The family member with the picture-perfect house may be drowning in debt. The artist whose work appears celebrated may feel creatively hollow. By measuring our insides against others' outsides, we build illusions that wound both confidence and connection.

RELATIONSHIPS WITHOUT RIVALRY

Comparison thrives on distance. It turns other people into objects against which we measure ourselves. Proximity dissolves that. It is hard to envy a neighbor's new car when you know the overtime that paid for it. It is hard to resent a friend's promotion when you've shared the late nights and setbacks that preceded it. Stories turn competitors into companions.

Escaping comparison also creates room for celebration. Instead of shrinking when friends flourish, you get to cheer. Connection deepens when success is shared, not shadowed.

There's a ripple effect. People relax around those who aren't keeping score. Performance gives way to presence. Homes and teams that practice gratitude over comparison feel warmer—and more honest.

Families benefit visibly. Parents who model

appreciation rather than envy teach children to value who they are, not what they display. Siblings become allies, not rivals. Couples stop measuring their relationship against an idealized feed and start nurturing the real one in front of them.

Communities flourish, too. Churches, workplaces, and neighborhoods shift from posturing to supporting. Energy once spent competing finds better use: cooperation, mutual aid, shared resources. Gifts become complementary rather than competitive.

Escaping comparison doesn't shrink achievement; it restores it. Success becomes contribution, not crowning.

PRACTICE: NAME AND REDIRECT

The next time envy strikes, pause for one deliberate breath. Then:

1. Name it

Acknowledge the comparison: "I feel jealous of their vacation/job/home."

2. Redirect it

Immediately write down or say aloud three things in your own life you value right now — however small.

3. Reframe it

Ask: "What does this show me about what I care about?" If it's travel, maybe it's the desire for adventure. If it's a promotion, maybe it's the desire for growth. This turns envy into information, not judgment.

With repetition, this short exercise interrupts the spiral before it deepens. Envy stops being a verdict and becomes a signal — one you can redirect toward gratitude and alignment.

THE STEADINESS OF ENOUGH

The most liberating gift of stepping out of comparison is stability. Self-worth stops rising and falling with someone else's fortunes. Life feels less like a seesaw and more like something anchored.

This steadiness isn't stagnation. You can still dream and build—you just do it from sufficiency rather than scarcity. The pursuit changes tone: less proving, more aligning. Joy returns to small victories—the project completed, the meal shared, the evening walk. Without someone else's highlight reel as the backdrop, everyday goodness is allowed to shine.

Stability also helps us weather change. Jobs shift, seasons turn, health wavers. If worth depends on staying ahead, every change threatens identity. If worth rests in sufficiency, loss may grieve us, but it does not define us. We remain whole, even when circumstances aren't.

Freedom follows. When you stop performing for perception, you stop curating life to impress. You arrange your days to feel aligned: meaningful, balanced, humane. That authenticity is lighter—and easier to sustain.

The whispers won't vanish; they are part of being human. Freedom is recognizing them early and choosing differently: notice, name, redirect—to gratitude, to values, to presence. Each redirection strengthens the muscle of peace.

Over time, what felt automatic becomes optional. The scoreboard recedes to background noise, and something sturdier takes its place: joy not contingent on others, but grounded in enough.

STEPPING OFF THE TREADMILL

Comparison often disguises itself as motivation: Look at them—do more, be more, have more. At first, it feels like fuel. In the long run, it's a loop. There will always be a "them," just out of reach.

Escaping takes courage—the courage to say, Enough of shaping my life around someone else's story. Enough of letting their abundance make mine feel small. This isn't withdrawal; it's liberation. You reclaim the energy spent on envy and invest it where it bears real fruit.

When comparison loosens, you don't lose ambition—you gain alignment. You don't lose connection—you deepen it. You don't lose joy—you recover it. Your life stops feeling like a lesser version of someone else's and starts feeling whole on its own terms.

Most importantly, you gain the freedom to live authentically. Worth is no longer a performance; it's a presence. The right people draw closer. Communities strengthen. Measurement gives way to meaning.

PRACTICES TO REFRAME

Escaping comparison requires not only awareness but action. Additional practices that expand the guardrails include:

1. Set personal baselines

Instead of gauging progress by others, choose baseline measures that belong to you. If running is your hobby, track your time against your own past records—not your neighbor's marathon medal. Growth becomes self-referential, not comparative.

2. Schedule comparison detoxes

Take intentional breaks from environments that trigger inadequacy—social media fasts, weekends without scrolling, months focused on offline pursuits. These detoxes clear mental space and reset perspective.

3. Reframe envy into aspiration

When someone's success stirs envy, ask: What about their achievement resonates with me? Instead of dwelling on lack, channel the feeling into inspiration.

4. Return to values in moments of wobble

Keep a short list—written or memorized—of your top values. When comparison strikes, revisit that list. Ask: Does this envy align with what matters to me, or am I chasing someone else's race?

Practice micro-gratitude in real time. When envy strikes in conversation—at the office, online, or in a social circle—immediately name one thing you value about your own current life. This disrupts the spiral before it deepens.

A BROADER REFLECTION

Comparison thrives because it preys on a universal desire: to know that we matter. Yet the truth is that significance isn't found in outrunning others. It is found in inhabiting our own story with integrity and presence. Every hour spent tallying someone else's life is an hour stolen from our own. Every ounce of energy devoted to keeping up could have been spent creating, loving, or resting. The trap isn't only that we feel inadequate—it's that we lose time, attention, and joy in the process.

When we begin to redirect that energy—toward gratitude, values, and authentic living—we don't merely escape something toxic; we reclaim something precious. We reclaim the freedom to notice our lives as they actually are. We reclaim the power to build on our own terms. We reclaim the quiet satisfaction of being enough.

Comparison won't disappear, and we don't need it to. What we need is clarity about the larger story that keeps it alive. Because comparison is personal, but it is also cultural. Powerful systems benefit when we are restless: advertising, consumerism, and corporate narratives thrive on our unease. If we're always measuring, we keep buying, upgrading, overworking.

That brings us to the next mirage: the corporate promise that more is always better, that growth is endless, that happiness sits just behind the next purchase or promotion. It is persuasive enough to shape not only individuals but entire societies—and, like comparison, it is built on scarcity.

In the next chapter, we will step back to examine how that mirage is made, why it keeps us chasing, and how to resist its grip. If comparison steals joy on the personal level, this story magnifies the theft at scale. Seeing both clearly is how we stay free.

CHAPTER NINE
THE CORPORATE MIRAGE

Step into almost any corporate boardroom and
you'll hear the same language repeated: *growth,
expansion, scaling, market share.* The unspoken
assumption is that more is always better—more
profit, more customers, more reach. It doesn't
matter if the company is already thriving; the
question is always, What's next? How do we get
bigger? This relentless pursuit of more is celebrated

as progress, but in truth, it is a mirage—a shimmering promise of fulfillment that recedes the closer we chase it.

The corporate world is built on the engine of perpetual dissatisfaction. Quarterly earnings must exceed the last. Productivity must outpace last year. Shareholders must be pleased with constant growth. This creates a culture where "enough" is never on the table. A company that makes steady, sufficient profits is seen not as stable, but as stagnant. The expectation of endless upward movement is so ingrained that slowing down is equated with failure.

This culture doesn't stay within boardrooms; it trickles down into our daily lives. Employees internalize the same language: performance reviews that demand constant improvement, goals that always escalate, incentives that reward more hours, more output, more availability. It's no longer enough to do good work; we're expected to exceed, outpace, outperform. The mirage isn't only for companies—it's for individuals, too.

And then there is advertising, the faithful partner of corporate growth. Companies know that expansion depends on restless consumers, so they cultivate that restlessness through marketing. You don't just need a phone; you need the newest phone. You don't just need clothes; you need this season's line. You don't just need food; you need the upgraded, premium, limited-edition version. The cycle is endless: corporations demand growth, growth demands consumers, and consumers are persuaded to feel perpetually behind.

But here's the reality: endless growth is unsustainable. Trees don't grow to the sky. Markets reach saturation. Resources are finite. And yet the mirage persists, shimmering on the horizon, urging us to believe that happiness lies in the next expansion. The irony is that in chasing it, both companies and individuals often erode the very stability they seek. Corporations collapse under the weight of unsustainable growth; workers burn out under the pressure of never being enough.

The tragedy of the corporate mirage is not only its illusion, but its cost. It reduces people to productivity, communities to markets, and the planet to resources. It feeds the myth that our worth is measured by output and possessions, not presence or purpose. It teaches us to equate busyness with success, expansion with progress, consumption with happiness. And in doing so, it blinds us to the possibility that enough is already here.

Escaping this mirage requires first recognizing it for what it is: not an inevitable truth, but a story we've been told. A story designed to keep us running—faster, harder, longer—without ever arriving.

THE MIRAGE AT WORK

The corporate obsession with growth doesn't remain abstract. It filters directly into the lives of the people who work within these systems. Careers, identities, and even personal values are shaped by the drumbeat of "more."

Consider the modern workplace. Employees are often told they are part of a "family," yet the loyalty expected rarely flows both ways. Bonuses, promotions, and praise are tied not to steady, sustainable performance but to exceeding expectations—to doing more than last year, taking on extra projects, stretching hours into nights and weekends. The unspoken truth is clear: your worth to the company is measured by output. And when you stop producing more, you risk being replaced.

I once met a project manager at a large tech firm who described her weeks as a blur of fourteen-hour days. Promotions and praise came quickly, but so did exhaustion. She admitted that she was terrified to take a weekend off, fearing she'd be labeled "uncommitted." When she finally collapsed from burnout and took medical leave, she said the most painful realization wasn't that she'd worked too hard — it was that the company replaced her within weeks. "I thought I was indispensable," she told me, "but I was just part of the machine."

This mindset seeps into how we define ourselves. We begin to equate self-worth with productivity. Rest feels like laziness. Saying "no" feels like failure. We carry the corporate mirage into our homes, measuring our days not by meaning but by metrics: emails sent, tasks completed, hours logged. Life becomes a to-do list, and the only acceptable score is "more."

The effect on time is equally corrosive. The workweek has expanded in ways previous generations could hardly imagine. With smartphones and laptops, the boundary between office and home has blurred to near extinction. We are always reachable, always "on," always expected to respond. Time that once belonged to family, hobbies, or rest is quietly absorbed by work. Even vacations are infiltrated—how many people now carry laptops to the beach or check emails at dinner? Corporate hunger doesn't respect personal boundaries; it devours them.

Even ambition itself is distorted. In its healthy form, ambition motivates growth, creativity, and contribution. But under the corporate mirage, ambition is warped into comparison and competition. Promotions are dangled like carrots, creating environments where colleagues become rivals rather than collaborators. Entire industries glorify the hustle, celebrating those who sacrifice health, relationships, and peace for the sake of advancement. The message is relentless: Do more, be more, earn more—or be left behind.

The irony is that this cycle often leaves people emptier, not fuller. Burnout is now a global epidemic, recognized by the World Health Organization as a workplace hazard.

Recent surveys back this up: nearly 77% of U.S. employees report experiencing burnout at their current job, and over half say it directly affects their sleep, relationships, or health. Globally, the International Labour Organization has linked long working hours to an estimated 745,000 deaths annually from stroke and heart disease.

Stress-related illnesses are on the rise. Workers report feeling disconnected, undervalued, and exhausted. And yet, many feel trapped—convinced that stepping back means falling behind in a race they can't afford to lose.

This is the personal cost of the corporate mirage. It convinces us that enough is never enough, that stability is stagnation, that worth must always be proven through more. And because this story is so widespread, many of us accept it as normal. We chase promotions that don't satisfy, buy products that don't fulfill, and live lives that feel busier but not better.

THE MANUFACTURED DISSATISFACTION

If the corporate machine depends on endless growth, then it also depends on one critical ingredient: our dissatisfaction. A satisfied consumer is a dangerous thing to the economy of "more." If we believe we have enough, we stop buying. If we feel content, we stop chasing. And so, industries have mastered the art of keeping us perpetually uneasy, subtly convinced that what we have—and who we are—is not quite enough.

Advertising is the most obvious tool. It doesn't just sell products; it sells discontent. Commercials rarely focus on what an item is—they focus on what it will supposedly make you. A car isn't just transportation; it's status, adventure, and freedom. A watch isn't just a timepiece; it's success, masculinity, or elegance. Shampoo isn't about clean hair; it's about being desirable. The message is clear: without this product, you are incomplete.

But dissatisfaction goes deeper than marketing campaigns. Entire industries are structured around planned obsolescence—designing products to wear out, break down, or fall behind trends quickly enough to demand replacement. Think of smartphones that slow down after a few years, fashion lines that cycle with each season, or appliances built with cheaper parts so they fail sooner. These aren't accidents; they are strategies. Contentment would stall profits, so discontent is engineered.

Social media amplifies this dissatisfaction to an unprecedented scale. Corporations harness algorithms that feed us a steady stream of curated lives, each image designed to stir longing. Vacation photos, luxury goods, fitness transformations—all presented as normal, all quietly urging us to want more. And because the ads themselves are woven into these feeds, we often don't even notice when our envy is being monetized. The line between authentic life and manufactured aspiration blurs, leaving us constantly chasing what others appear to have.

Even language is weaponized. "New and improved," "limited edition," "exclusive offer"— these phrases aren't just descriptors, they are triggers. They create urgency, a fear of missing out, a sense that without this purchase we will be left behind. And the more often we hear them, the more normal they sound. Soon, we equate consumption with progress, buying with belonging.

The result is a culture of quiet anxiety. Even when our needs are met, we feel restless. Even when we're surrounded by abundance, we feel deprived. And this is not by accident—it is by design. The corporate mirage depends on keeping us thirsty, no matter how much we drink.

THE BROADER COSTS

The corporate mirage doesn't only exhaust individuals; it strains entire systems—social, economic, and ecological. The pursuit of "more" ripples outward, creating consequences that touch communities and the planet itself.

On a human level, endless growth has reshaped the workplace into a breeding ground for stress. The World Health Organization now identifies burnout as an occupational phenomenon, and rates of anxiety and depression tied to overwork continue to climb globally. Employees are encouraged to sacrifice sleep, family, and health in service of productivity metrics that never stop moving. What was once framed as ambition is now recognized as unsustainable. Yet the culture persists, driven by shareholders who demand more and companies that compete for dominance.

The costs are also economic. A system built on consumption depends on debt to fuel it. Credit cards, financing plans, "buy now, pay later" schemes—all designed to keep people purchasing beyond their means. The corporate machine thrives when individuals stay just far enough behind to need the next paycheck, the next loan, the next promotion. The mirage is not only about wanting more, but about being trapped in cycles of dependency.

Then there are the environmental costs, perhaps the most sobering of all. An economy that requires endless production inevitably collides with the limits of a finite planet. Fast fashion alone produces millions of tons of textile waste each year, much of it destined for landfills or incineration.

To put it in perspective: the fashion industry is responsible for roughly 10% of global carbon emissions, more than international flights and shipping combined. Electronics are equally sobering: the world produces over 50 million metric tons of e-waste annually, much of it containing toxic metals that leach into soil and water.

Electronics designed for obsolescence contribute to mountains of toxic e-waste. Resource extraction—for oil, minerals, timber—continues at unsustainable rates, degrading ecosystems and fueling climate change. The mirage insists on growth without end, but nature does not bend to that story.

Communities also feel the strain. Local shops and craftspeople struggle to compete with corporate giants who profit by scaling cheaply and aggressively. Small towns hollow out when factories relocate overseas in search of lower costs.

In one small western Massachusetts town, I visited a family-run hardware store that had been in business for three generations. The owners knew their customers by name and often extended informal credit when times were tight. But when a national big-box chain opened just ten miles away, sales plummeted. Within a year, the store closed, leaving not just a vacant building but a hole in the town's social fabric. "It wasn't just a store," a longtime customer said. "It was where neighbors met, where advice was shared, where trust lived. The chain sells the same tools, but it doesn't replace that."

Workers become numbers on a spreadsheet, valued for efficiency rather than humanity. The relentless push for expansion rarely pauses to ask: Who is being left behind? Who pays the price?

Even our cultural values shift under the weight of the mirage. Where once success might have been measured by integrity, craftsmanship, or contribution to community, it is now too often equated with scale. Bigger becomes synonymous with better, regardless of quality. The artisan loses to mass production, the thoughtful creator to the fastest trend. In such a climate, the quiet virtues of sufficiency are drowned out by the noise of accumulation.

The irony is sharp: in chasing endless growth, corporations often undermine the very foundations that make growth possible. Overworked employees burn out and leave. Debt-burdened consumers eventually stop spending. A degraded environment can no longer yield the resources demanded of it. The mirage shimmers, but it hides a desert underneath.

RESISTING THE MIRAGE

Seeing the corporate mirage for what it is—an illusion built on endless growth and manufactured dissatisfaction—is only the first step. The harder task is choosing to live differently in a culture that rewards compliance. Resistance, in this context, doesn't mean rejecting work or commerce altogether. It means reclaiming agency, redefining success, and refusing to let the story of "more" dictate the story of our lives.

One way to resist is by redefining success on personal terms. Corporations measure growth in quarterly profits; individuals can measure growth in alignment with values. Instead of asking, Did I get promoted? Did I earn more? we ask, Did I spend time on what matters? Did I contribute in a way that feels meaningful? Did I protect my health and relationships? These questions shift the focus from external approval to internal integrity.

Another act of resistance is embracing sufficiency in consumption. Companies thrive on convincing us that happiness is a transaction. But we can weaken that system by choosing intentionally: buying less, repairing instead of replacing, supporting local businesses instead of global giants. Each act may seem small, but collectively they erode the power of a culture built on waste. Every time we choose "enough," we push back against the machinery of "more."

Communities can also resist by prioritizing cooperation over competition. Neighborhood tool libraries, community gardens, clothing swaps, and co-ops are quiet revolutions against corporate isolation. They remind us that abundance doesn't always mean ownership; it often means sharing. In a world where corporations pit us against each other as consumers, collaboration is a radical statement of sufficiency.

At work, resistance might mean setting boundaries. Refusing to equate availability with value. Protecting evenings, weekends, and vacations from encroachment. Speaking openly about burnout. These choices are rarely easy in environments that reward overwork, but they create ripples. They model a different way of being, one that values people as more than productivity.

A 7-DAY RESET FOR ENOUGHNESS

Think of this as a small, humane experiment in shifting attention away from corporate pressure and toward sufficiency.

Day 1 — Audit.

Identify your top three "mirage triggers" (apps, workplace rituals, marketing messages). Just notice.

Day 2 — Subtract.

Unsubscribe from one email campaign, mute two ads or accounts. Create micro-silence.

Day 3 — Replace.

Add one nourishing input—a book, a long walk, or even a conversation that isn't about work or consumption.

Day 4 — Boundary.

Choose one daily "off" window (e.g., 7–9pm). Devices down, corporate demands paused.

Day 5 — Gratitude in the Wild.

When envy strikes, name one sufficiency you already have: "Right now I have health, shelter, or peace of mind."

Day 6 — Progress, not proof.

Do one act that aligns with values (volunteer, craft, rest). Note how it felt, not how it looked.

Day 7 — Review.

What subtraction mattered most? Which addition lifted your energy? Keep those.

These micro-shifts won't dismantle corporate culture, but they will loosen its grip on you. They remind you that sufficiency is possible—and that agency still belongs to you.

Before moving forward, take five minutes to recall the last time you felt pressured to say yes to "more" — a project at work, a purchase, a commitment you weren't sure about. Ask yourself: What did that choice cost me in energy, time, or peace? What did I truly gain? Write it down. Seeing the trade-off on paper often reveals whether the mirage is pulling you forward, or whether sufficiency would have served you better.

RECLAIMING AMBITION

Escaping the corporate mirage doesn't mean abandoning ambition. It means reclaiming it. Ambition in its healthiest form is about growth, contribution, and creativity. It's the desire to stretch our abilities, to build something meaningful, to leave the world a little better than we found it. That kind of ambition is not the problem. The problem is when ambition is hijacked by the narrative of "more."

Corporate culture tells us that ambition should always point upward: higher titles, larger salaries, bigger offices, wider reach. But there are other directions. Ambition can also point inward—toward greater depth of character, stronger relationships, richer inner lives. It can point outward—toward service, community, or the environment. It can point toward balance rather than expansion. Ambition doesn't have to be about climbing a ladder; it can be about planting deeper roots.

When we strip ambition of comparison, it becomes liberating. A teacher's ambition might be to inspire curiosity in her students, not to earn accolades. A craftsman's ambition might be to refine his skill, not to mass-produce. A parent's ambition might be to raise kind children, not to showcase a picture-perfect family. These ambitions are no less worthy than corporate ones—in fact, they often lead to more lasting impact.

THREE AMBITION REFRAMES

1) From Ladder to Lattice.

Old script: up or out.

New frame: growth can move across (skills, scope, craft).

Micro-move: *shadow a colleague in a different discipline, or trade prestige for balance.*

2) From Audience to Impact.

Old script: success = visibility.

New frame: success = usefulness.

Micro-move: *keep an "impact log"—a short weekly list of who benefited from your work.*

3) From Pace to Rhythm.

Old script: faster is better.

New frame: sustainable beats sensational.

Micro-move: *set one cadence ritual—Focus Fridays, no-meeting mornings, or a weekly digital sabbath.*

Reframing ambition doesn't shrink your world; it re-centers it. The astonishing thing is how results often improve when you stop sprinting for optics and start moving for meaning.

CHOOSING BETTER

The corporate mirage is persuasive because it plays to something deeply human: the desire for security, recognition, and progress. But the tragedy is that it promises these things while simultaneously undermining them. Security is replaced with instability, because "enough" is never allowed. Recognition is fleeting, because accomplishments are always measured against the next goal. Progress becomes endless motion with no destination. Like a desert traveler chasing a shimmer on the horizon, we run harder and harder, only to find that the water we long for was never there.

The truth is simple but radical: there is no finish line in the story of "more." Corporations cannot define when we are satisfied, complete, or successful. Only we can. The moment we stop measuring our worth by quarterly reports, job titles, or consumption levels, we step out of the illusion. We begin to tell a different story—one that values sufficiency over scarcity, quality over quantity, and meaning over metrics.

This doesn't mean abandoning work, business, or even growth itself. It means refusing to let them dominate the definition of a good life. Work has value when it sustains us, contributes to others, and expresses our gifts. Growth has value when it aligns with our values, not when it drags us into endless restlessness. Consumption has value when it meets real needs, not when it fuels dissatisfaction. The shift is subtle but profound: from chasing more to choosing what matters.

Breaking free of the corporate mirage requires courage. It often means resisting expectations, declining opportunities that don't align, or walking away from environments that demand constant sacrifice. But the reward is worth it: a life that feels grounded, intentional, and free. We can choose to stop running toward the shimmer and start building something real where we already stand.

A CLOSING PRACTICE

If you remember only one thing, let it be this: the mirage loses power every time you choose attention over appetite. Once a week, sit somewhere ordinary—kitchen table, bus seat, park bench—and list ten sufficiencies within arm's reach. Not dreams; already-heres. A repaired chair. A paid bill. A neighbor's hello. The smell of coffee. Sun warming a wall. Ten is hard the first time; by week three it gets easier. This is not naïveté. It is training. You are teaching your mind to recognize water when the desert insists there is none.

The corporate mirage is powerful, but it is not unbreakable. And as we begin to live differently, we inevitably notice something else: the role of people in shaping our stories. Corporate culture may pressure us, but often it is individuals—bosses, colleagues, friends, even family—who reinforce the myth of more in our daily lives. Some relationships nurture us, encouraging gratitude, presence, and sufficiency. Others drain us, keeping us stuck in comparison, competition, or scarcity.

This brings us to the next crucial step: relationships. If the corporate mirage shows how systems can trap us, then our personal connections reveal how people can either free us or hold us back. To live in alignment with enough, we must learn not only how to cultivate gratitude, but also how to discern which relationships are healthy and which are toxic—and sometimes, how to let go.

In the next chapter, we will explore what it means to move from rivalry to relationship. We'll talk about the power of surrounding ourselves with people who encourage contentment and joy—and the necessity of stepping away from those who thrive on negativity, comparison, and scarcity. Because finding sunshine isn't only about changing our habits. It's also about choosing the company we keep.

CHAPTER TEN
RELATIONSHIPS NOT RIVALRIES

If gratitude steadies us and comparison unsettles us, then relationships are the stage where both forces collide. The people we surround ourselves with either nurture a sense of enough or keep us endlessly chasing more. Relationships are never neutral; they shape how we see ourselves, how we spend our time, and what we believe life should look like.

Joy multiplies when shared—but so can discontent. A friend's encouragement can make a modest victory feel radiant. A colleague's subtle rivalry can make the same achievement feel small. A family gathering can affirm the beauty of simple living or stir anxiety about not measuring up. Our connections act as mirrors, reflecting sufficiency or scarcity.

Many of us live among relationships that lean toward rivalry instead of connection. Some of these pressures are unintentional—friends swept along by consumer culture, family members who equate success with possessions, coworkers who compete because they feel they must. Others are deliberate—people who thrive on criticism, diminish others to elevate themselves, or measure worth by status. These dynamics corrode peace and reinforce the myth that we are never enough.

The difficulty is that toxicity rarely declares itself. It slips in through familiarity or obligation: a friend who cloaks critique in "just being honest," a colleague who disguises rivalry as playful banter, a relative whose "advice" is really pressure to conform. Over time, these patterns tether us to the chase for validation.

Healthy relationships point us elsewhere. They invite us to celebrate what we already have instead of fixating on what we lack. They grant permission to rest, to say no, to pursue alignment instead of relentless achievement. They remind us we are valued not for what we own or produce but for who we are. These connections don't spark rivalry; they build resilience.

The truth is plain: finding sunshine depends on choosing the company we keep. Just as clutter crowds out peace in a home, relational clutter crowds out joy. And just as decluttering begins with noticing what no longer serves us, relational health begins with discerning which connections sustain and which ones drain.

This isn't a demand for flawless people—every relationship has rough edges. It is a call to draw boundaries with those who consistently bring negativity, comparison, or manipulation, and sometimes to step away entirely. In the same way living with less creates space for gratitude, stepping back from toxic ties creates space for healthier ones to grow.

SEEING CLEARLY

I once knew someone who seemed endlessly supportive—always quick with advice, always ready with an opinion. At first, I mistook it for care. But over time, I noticed a pattern: their "encouragement" left me doubting myself, questioning choices I had felt good about before the conversation. What I thought was guidance was really control dressed as concern. It wasn't until I stepped back that I realized how much lighter life felt without that constant undertone of criticism. Sometimes toxicity doesn't shout; it whispers, slowly eroding our confidence until distance reveals the difference.

We often sense when a connection feels heavy but struggle to name why. Without language, we normalize toxicity: that's just how they are or I shouldn't be so sensitive. Clarity matters. When we can identify patterns, we gain the power to respond with intention.

COMMON SIGNS OF TOXIC RELATIONSHIPS

1. Constant criticism.

Feedback builds when it's constructive; toxic critique diminishes. If you routinely leave interactions feeling smaller or perpetually wrong, pay attention.

2. Competition disguised as connection.

Healthy ambition inspires; rivalry exhausts. One-upping isn't celebration—it's scorekeeping.

3. Conditional support.

In nurturing bonds, care remains steady. Toxic ties help only when it benefits them, or when you conform.

4. Energy drain.

After time together, do you feel lighter or depleted? Our bodies often register toxicity before our minds rationalize it.

5. Manipulation or guilt.

Twisted words, guilt trips, and being made responsible for another's mood are not care; they're control.

6. Boundary blindness.

Repeated disregard for limits—about time, topics, or tone—signals misalignment.

MARKERS OF LIFE GIVING RELATIONSHIPS

1. Encouragement without competition.

They celebrate your victories as if they were their own.

2. Room for authenticity.

You can bring joys, struggles, and imperfections without fear.

3. Consistency.

Support doesn't vanish when you falter.

4.Mutuality.

The flow of effort balances over time.

5. Respect for boundaries.

Your "no" is honored without punishment.

Identifying these patterns isn't about labeling people as good or bad; it's about acknowledging impact. A relationship can include kindness and still leave you drained. Another can host disagreements and still be deeply supportive. What matters is direction: does this relationship nurture your search for enough, or pull you back into the myth of more?

Clarity may reveal truths we'd rather avoid: a friend whose negativity has become corrosive, a family member whose expectations stifle, a colleague whose competitiveness erodes trust. Seeing clearly doesn't require cutting ties immediately, but it does require honesty about what is happening. Awareness is the beginning of choice—and choice is the foundation of freedom.

BOUNDARIES THAT PROTECT PEACE

Many fear boundaries because they mistake them for rejection. In reality, boundaries are respect—for ourselves and often for the relationship itself. They define what is acceptable, what is not, and how we will engage. Without them, resentment festers; with them, clarity emerges.

Boundaries don't always mean cutting people off. Sometimes they mean adjusting access. You may still love a friend but limit time together. You may remain close to a family member while refusing topics that always end in conflict. You may work alongside a colleague while declining their competitive games. Boundaries are not punishment; they are protection.

Not every connection can be preserved. Some are so draining or manipulative that the healthiest choice is to let go. This is painful—especially where history or obligation run deep—but holding on out of guilt prolongs harm. Letting go can be an act of self-respect and, at times, compassion, freeing both people from a cycle that no longer serves either of you.

Letting go doesn't require hostility. Often it looks like a quiet shift: responding less, declining invitations, gently stepping back until the bond loosens. In other cases—especially with persistent boundary violations—it means being direct: "I value our history, and this no longer feels healthy for me."

The fear, of course, is loneliness. We worry that releasing toxic ties will leave us empty. Paradoxically, letting go creates space. Just as clearing a room makes space for peace, releasing draining relationships makes space for healthier ones to grow. The absence is not emptiness—it is possibility.

Some relationships are for a season; clinging after the season ends only creates pain. Others may transform when boundaries are introduced. Still others fade once we stop feeding the rivalry that sustained them. Protecting your peace is not selfish; it's necessary. A life rooted in sufficiency cannot flourish if it is constantly poisoned by voices insisting you are not enough.

To make boundaries more tangible, try experimenting with simple practices:

1. The Relationship Audit.

Once a month, list the people you spend most time with. Note who leaves you energized and who leaves you depleted. Adjust your calendar accordingly.

2. The Weekly "No."

Choose one small request each week you will decline kindly but firmly. It's not rejection—it's practice in protecting peace.

3. The Honest Pause.

When someone's words sting, ask yourself: "Did this feel like support, or did it feel like pressure?" That moment of clarity often reveals whether a boundary is needed.

BUILDING WHAT BRINGS LIFE

Releasing toxicity is only half the work. The more joyful half is cultivating relationships that bring life, light, and resilience. These connections remind us of what matters, reflect our best selves, and anchor us in sufficiency when the world tempts us toward more.

Life-giving relationships rarely arrive with fanfare. They show up as quiet consistency: the friend who listens without fixing, the neighbor who checks in, the mentor who believes in you when you're unsure. These are the people who leave you lighter, who remind you that being yourself is enough.

Three qualities sit at the heart of nurturing bonds:

1. Trust.

You can be vulnerable without fear of betrayal.

2. Encouragement.

They see your potential and cheer you on without turning success into competition.

3. Presence.

They show up—not only when things go well, but also when life is messy.

Cultivating such relationships requires intentionality. We can't simply wait for them to appear; we must nurture them like gardens. Reach out even when life is busy. Practice honesty rather than hiding behind politeness. Offer support first instead of waiting to be asked. Strong bonds are built through small, consistent acts of care.

They also require reciprocity. If we want others to listen, we must listen. If we want encouragement, we must offer it. If we want presence, we must show up. Balance doesn't mean perfect equality—some seasons we give more; other seasons we receive more—but over time both people feel nourished, not emptied.

Shared values add stability. Relationships rooted in kindness, simplicity, integrity, or generosity feel steady because they rest on a common foundation. Differences bring richness, but aligned values make connection resilient.

Vulnerability is essential. After toxic dynamics, it is tempting to keep interactions shallow, to avoid risk. But deep connection requires being seen. Vulnerability may feel risky; it is also the gateway to intimacy and trust.

As we invest in these bonds, something shifts. We no longer cling to toxic ties out of fear of being alone. We discover that companionship grows from presence, not performance. The search for sunshine becomes a shared journey.

A former colleague once called me out of the blue after hearing I had finished a major project. There was no angle, no competition, no "but have you thought about..."—just a genuine, "I'm proud of you. That's a big deal." That one call reminded me how powerful it is to have people who celebrate without keeping score. Encouragement like that doesn't just affirm the achievement—it affirms the person.

THE WIDER NET: COMMUNITY

Research reinforces what intuition already knows. A long-running study at Harvard found that close relationships—not wealth, fame, or achievement—are the strongest predictors of long-term happiness and health. Another meta-analysis by psychologist Julianne Holt-Lunstad showed that loneliness increases the risk of premature death by 26%. The science is clear: healthy connection is not just a nice addition to life; it is a cornerstone of survival.

Individual relationships shape our daily lives, but community creates the atmosphere where our sense of "enough" either thrives or withers.

Communities can unintentionally fuel rivalry. Think of workplaces where collaboration is overshadowed by competition for promotions, or social groups where subtle status markers—cars, vacations, square footage—become scoreboards. Even faith communities, meant to model grace and generosity, sometimes slip into tallying who appears the most "together." In such spaces, worth feels external: valued for what we produce, perform, or possess.

Yet community can also be the antidote. When groups prioritize cooperation, sufficiency flourishes. A neighborhood that shares tools or watches children. A workplace that rewards collaboration alongside results. A friend group that celebrates milestones without turning them into benchmarks. These environments remind us we belong—and that belonging isn't earned by more; it is given through connection.

A helpful shift is moving from transactional to transformational communities. Transactional groups revolve around exchange: I give to get. Transformational groups center on growth: we give because we care, and we receive because we belong. Scarcity rules the former; abundance emerges in the latter.

Creating such spaces is intentional. Start a book club where honesty outranks pretense. Join a volunteer effort where contribution is measured in care, not status. Commit to family dinners as gatherings of presence, not showcases of perfection. What matters is that these practices reinforce sufficiency.

Communities also safeguard us when toxic individuals or systems threaten peace. A strong network can counterbalance a draining person or a competitive workplace. They remind us who we are when other voices insist we are not enough. In this way, healthy communities anchor us when the world pulls toward restlessness.

The beauty is in the spillover. When we invest in life-giving communities, we multiply our choices. One person's decision to live with enough inspires another's. Gratitude spreads. Simplicity becomes contagious. Joy is shared. The search for sunshine becomes a collective movement toward sufficiency.

So the question isn't only, Who are my friends? but also, What kind of community am I building? Relationships shape individuals; communities shape cultures. The culture we create together determines whether rivalry thrives—or resilience does.

COMPANIONS FOR A COUNTER-CULTURAL LIFE

Living with less, embracing gratitude, and

resisting comparison are powerful practices—but hard to sustain in isolation. Alone, we are vulnerable to old patterns and the relentless pull of culture. With the right people beside us, we find strength. Relationships and communities become the scaffolding that supports the life we're building.

Think of swimming against a current alone versus moving with a group. On your own, the struggle is exhausting. With companions, the effort lightens and the pace steadies. That's what supportive relationships do: they ease the weight of countercultural living and remind us we are not foolish for rejecting the chase for more—we are wise, and we are not alone.

This is why investing in life-giving relationships isn't just about personal well-being; it's about resilience. A friend who values simplicity will cheer your choice not to upgrade your phone rather than tease you for "falling behind." A mentor who understands balance will applaud protecting family time rather than pushing you to sacrifice it for advancement. A community that honors authenticity will embrace imperfections rather than demand polish. These voices counter the cultural chorus of "more, more, more" with a gentler refrain: enough, enough, enough.

Healthy relationships also keep us accountable in ways toxic ones never could. When we drift toward comparison, supportive friends remind us what matters. When we're tempted by overconsumption, communities rooted in simplicity help us remember why we chose this path. Accountability here isn't judgment; it's encouragement—a shared commitment to live differently, together.

Most importantly, relationships and community give us joy along the way. Minimalism and sufficiency are not grim disciplines but celebrations of freedom. Joy grows when shared: a potluck with neighbors, a family evening free from screens, a community project that makes life better for everyone involved. Such moments remind us that the sunshine we seek is often found in connection itself, not in acquisition.

Even healthy communities have missteps. Frustrations and misunderstandings will come. But when the foundation is trust, encouragement, and shared values, challenges become opportunities for growth rather than reasons for rivalry.

In the end, relationships and community are not extras on the journey toward enough; they are essentials. They provide belonging no possession can replace, encouragement no advertisement can manufacture, and stability no corporate ladder can guarantee. When toxic connections fall away, the space left behind is not emptiness but invitation—an opening for relationships that nourish rather than drain, for communities that inspire rather than exhaust.

CHOOSING THE COMPANY WE KEEP

The people around us shape not only how we live but how we see ourselves. They can nudge us toward sufficiency or pull us back into scarcity. They can magnify gratitude or magnify envy. They can encourage us to slow down and savor, or push us to keep sprinting toward the mirage of "more." In many ways, our search for sunshine rises or falls with the company we keep.

Letting go of toxic relationships isn't merely self-protection; it's alignment. By stepping away from those who drain us, diminish us, or tether us to comparison, we honor that our time and energy are finite. Every hour spent with someone who poisons our peace is an hour stolen from joy. Every boundary drawn, every tie released, is space reclaimed for what truly matters.

Equally, nurturing life-giving relationships is essential. These connections remind us, again and again, that we are not alone in resisting excess. They help us believe, when doubt creeps in, that enough really is enough. They cheer simplicity, celebrate without rivalry, and anchor us in authenticity. With such people beside us, sufficiency is no longer a lonely experiment but a shared way of living.

Communities extend this impact exponentially. One friend's encouragement is powerful; a network of encouragement is transformative. When groups commit to valuing presence over performance, cooperation over competition, and sufficiency over scarcity, they create environments where living with less feels natural rather than strange. Those environments ripple outward, shaping families, workplaces, and cultures.

We were never meant to do this alone. Human beings are wired for connection. When those connections are rooted in respect, gratitude, and authenticity, they become the fertile ground where joy can take root and grow.

As we move forward, we'll apply these truths not only to people but to our way of living itself. For while relationships shape us, so do our possessions, habits, and choices about what we keep and what we release. Having learned to curate the company we keep, we must now learn to curate the lives we lead.

Take a sheet of paper and divide it in two columns: Life-Giving and Life-Draining. Write three names in each. Don't overthink—just notice who comes to mind. Then ask: How can I spend one more hour this week with those in the first column? And what is one step—however small—I can take to loosen the hold of someone in the second? The practice isn't about judgment; it's about choosing alignment.

In the next chapter, we turn to the art of living with less. Minimalism is not deprivation; it is freedom. Choosing less creates space for more of what matters: presence, peace, and joy. The external act of decluttering mirrors the internal work of simplifying our hearts. Relationships have shown us that abundance is found in connection, not competition. Now we'll see how the same truth applies to the material world: abundance is not in accumulation, but in sufficiency.

CHAPTER ELEVEN

THE ART OF LESS:
COMPOSITION OVER ACCUMULATION

Living with less is not only a choice—it's a craft. Like an artist with a canvas, we decide what belongs and what distracts, what enhances the picture and what clutters it. Minimalism, in this sense, is not about stripping life bare. It's about arranging it with intention so that what remains creates beauty, meaning, and balance.

This is why living with less can be called an art.

Art is never only about the materials; it's about the expression. A painter does not use fewer colors for the sake of austerity—they choose a palette for harmony. A musician doesn't avoid notes merely to prove restraint—they compose melodies that leave space for silence. In the same way, minimalism is not simply about owning fewer things; it's about shaping life so that what remains resonates.

The art of living with less begins with perspective. Instead of asking, What do I need to remove? we ask, What do I want to highlight? A minimalist home, for example, isn't about empty rooms; it's about rooms that reflect what matters— a well-loved chair by a sunny window, a table where meals and conversations unfold, a shelf with books that have shaped you. The absence of excess creates space for presence.

This applies beyond possessions. In our schedules, the art of less means curating time for what truly matters. It might mean fewer commitments but deeper involvement. Instead of scattering energy across endless obligations, we choose the ones that bring meaning. A calendar with intentional whitespace is not laziness; it is artistry—leaving room for breath, spontaneity, and rest.

In habits, too, the art of less is powerful. Consider the rituals that start and end your day. Many of us fill these spaces with noise—checking phones, rushing, cramming tasks. The art of less asks: What single practice could transform this moment? A quiet cup of tea. A few lines in a journal. A short walk at dusk. These small, deliberate rituals shape life with the same precision a sculptor uses to reveal form—removing what is unnecessary so the essential can be seen.

The beauty of this approach is that it shifts minimalism from restriction to creativity. Instead of obsessing over how little we can own or how much we can cut away, we focus on what kind of life we want to design. Less becomes not an end in itself, but the means by which we make space for meaning.

Like any art form, this takes practice. No one expects a painter to create a masterpiece the first time they touch a brush. Likewise, we don't master living with less overnight. We experiment, adjust, and refine. Sometimes we remove too much and feel deprived. Sometimes we keep too much and feel cluttered. The art lies in finding balance and in treating the process itself as part of the beauty.

Living with less, when seen as art, becomes less

about sacrifice and more about composition. It is not about emptying life, but about arranging it—so that what remains is enough, and enough feels abundant.

When minimalism is treated as art, every area of life becomes a canvas. Each choice—what to own, how to spend time, which habits to keep—contributes to the picture we are painting. The goal isn't perfection, but coherence. Life begins to feel less like a chaotic collage and more like a work in progress with direction and flow.

POSSESSIONS:

CURATE, DON'T JUST CUT

Possessions are often the first layer of the canvas because they're visible. Yet the artistry isn't just in discarding what you don't need; it's in curating what you keep. Imagine opening a closet where every item fits, feels good, and reflects your style. The experience is lighter, calmer, even joyful—not because of how much is gone, but because of how well what remains belongs. The art is not the emptiness of space, but the harmony of what's left.

A simple exercise: choose a single shelf or

drawer and ask only three questions—Does it serve? Does it fit? Does it delight? Keep what earns a yes to at least two. Notice how the whole room feels different when one small place is composed with care. Minimalism is fractal: arrange one corner, and the pattern spreads.

Vignette: A chipped ceramic bowl sits on the counter. It's not the prettiest, but it's the one your grandmother used to hold lemons. You could replace it with something more modern, but the bowl anchors dinners and memories. The art of less keeps the bowl—not out of sentimentality alone, but because it holds a story you still live inside.

TIME:

COMPOSE A RHYTHM

Time is another canvas, though less tangible. Here, artistry comes from rhythm. Think of a schedule not as a grid to be filled, but as music to be composed. Too many notes—too many commitments—create noise. Too few, and the melody feels sparse. The art is in balance: enough structure to give life shape, enough openness to leave room for breath. Some people find this by carving out "white space" on the calendar, protecting it as fiercely as any meeting. Others design recurring rituals—a weekly meal with family, a monthly hike with friends, an annual day of solitude. The point is not to have less activity, but to arrange activity with care, so that time feels like rhythm rather than racket.

Try this: circle three "signature moments" you want each week to include. They might be breakfast at the table, a midweek walk, or an hour of uninterrupted reading. Guard those moments. When the week threatens to swell, let the signatures hold the shape.

DAILY RITUALS:

THE BRUSH STROKES

Daily rituals are where the art of less becomes intimate. These are the brushstrokes of ordinary life. A morning routine can be heavy with obligations—checking messages, skimming news, rushing—or it can be simple and intentional: stretching, savoring a quiet moment, setting one clear intention. The difference is not time but attention. In the art of less, rituals are designed not for efficiency alone, but for nourishment.

Evenings offer another canvas for rhythm. Too often, they are consumed by screens, emails, or exhaustion. But when treated as an art, evenings can be designed to close the day with calm. Reading a few pages of a book, sharing a meal without distractions, walking outside as the light fades— these practices gently signal that the day is complete. They create space for rest to begin.

Seasonal rituals matter, too. Many traditional cultures were shaped by the cycles of planting and harvest, light and darkness, activity and rest. Modern life flattens these rhythms, treating every season as identical—always busy, always productive. Minimalism restores cadence: winter as a time of consolidation, spring as emergence, summer as abundance, fall as letting go. Recognizing these patterns allows us to live more in tune with nature and with ourselves.

CREATIVITY AND CONSTRAINT

Even creativity benefits from this approach. Writers, musicians, and artists know that constraints often spark innovation. A poet working within the limits of a haiku, a composer using only a few instruments, a painter choosing a narrow palette—these boundaries do not stifle creativity; they refine it. In the same way, living with less forces us to see abundance in what's already here. A simple meal, made with care, becomes a feast. A modest home, arranged with warmth, becomes a sanctuary. Fewer tools, fewer options, fewer distractions—paradoxically, these create more depth, not less.

Consider a maker's studio pared back to the essentials: a sturdy table, a good lamp, a small set of trusted tools. The space doesn't announce brilliance; it allows it. Constraint reduces friction. When the choice is clear, the work can begin.

ADAPTIVE NOT RIGID

What makes this practice unique is that it resists rigidity. It's not about strict rules—"own 100 items," "follow a minimalist diet," "never buy new things." Those approaches often collapse under their own weight. The art of living with less is not prescriptive but adaptive. It allows each person to shape their life according to their values, creating coherence rather than conformity.

Think of it as a living composition. The piece shifts when the season shifts: a newborn, a new job, an illness, a return to school. The art of less flexes with reality rather than breaking against it. Your canvas changes; so does your palette.

INNER MINIMALISM:
CLEARING THE MIND

If the art of living with less begins with possessions and time, its truest power unfolds in the mind. Our homes may be tidy, our schedules balanced, but if our thoughts remain crowded and chaotic, we still carry clutter wherever we go. Mental and emotional minimalism is the often-overlooked frontier—a way of clearing space within so that peace and clarity can flourish.

Consider how much mental noise fills an ordinary day: reminders of unfinished tasks, echoes of conversations we replay, worries about the future, comparisons scrolling through our minds like ticker tape. Much of this is invisible, yet it weighs as heavily as any overstuffed closet. Decluttering the mind begins with awareness—

noticing what thoughts serve us and what thoughts simply take up space.

One practical way to practice this is a thought inventory. As we might sort a drawer, we pause to observe what we're carrying. Which thoughts bring clarity, direction, or encouragement? Which stir only anxiety or resentment? The goal isn't to eliminate all negative thoughts—they're human—but to stop giving endless space to those that deplete without offering growth.

Another element of mental minimalism is reducing inputs. The human brain wasn't designed to process thousands of headlines, updates, and notifications each day. When we flood our minds with constant information, we leave no room for reflection. The art of less invites us to curate what we consume: fewer news cycles, fewer social feeds, fewer empty distractions. In that silence, creativity and calm have space to rise.

Emotional clutter requires attention as well. Many of us carry grudges, regrets, or unresolved conflicts that occupy mental real estate. These weights are not always easy to release, but holding them indefinitely is like leaving old boxes piled in the corner of the heart. Forgiveness—of ourselves and of others—becomes a form of decluttering. It doesn't erase the past; it loosens the grip of resentment so joy can move in.

Practices like journaling, a brief daily meditation, or a quiet walk can help here. Writing down lingering worries unburdens the mind the way hauling out trash clears a room. Sitting still, even for a few minutes, helps us notice the chatter we've mistaken for truth. These small acts are not indulgences; they are tools of inner minimalism, clearing the clutter that clouds presence.

The art of less, applied within, is not about chasing constant serenity. It's about creating enough space for peace to have a chance. A cluttered mind leaves no room for gratitude; a cluttered heart leaves no room for joy. When we lighten the load within, we carry ourselves differently—calmer, clearer, and more open to the sunshine already around us.

In the end, external minimalism is incomplete without its internal counterpart. We can declutter homes and schedules endlessly, but unless we declutter the mind and heart, the weight of excess will follow us wherever we go.

RELATIONAL MINIMALISM:
CONNECTION WITHOUT NOISE

Minimalism in relationships doesn't mean fewer people in our lives—it means more intentional connection. Just as clutter crowds our homes, unnecessary noise can crowd our conversations and interactions. The art of less in relationships removes what distracts from real connection so authenticity can take center stage.

One form of relational clutter is performative interaction. We've all been in conversations that feel like rehearsed scripts: polite small talk, exaggerated updates meant to impress, subtle competitions about who is busier, more stressed, more accomplished. These exchanges drain because they skim the surface without touching depth. Practicing relational minimalism means letting go of the need to perform—choosing honesty and presence instead. A simple, "I've been tired lately, but here's what I'm grateful for," creates more connection than a polished but hollow monologue.

Another form of clutter is overcommitment. Many of us fill our calendars with obligations more about keeping up appearances than nurturing relationships. We attend gatherings that leave us exhausted, say yes out of guilt, and spread ourselves so thin that none of our connections receive real attention. The art of less asks us to pause: Am I saying yes out of desire or duty? Fewer commitments allow us to be fully present in the ones that matter.

Communication itself can be simplified. We often believe we need the right words, long explanations, or elaborate gestures to show care. But connection thrives on simplicity: a sincere word, a handwritten note, a moment of undivided attention. Listening deeply—without planning our reply, without checking our phones, without judgment—is one of the purest forms of relational minimalism. It costs nothing and communicates everything.

There's also a role for boundaries here, as in the previous chapter. Overexplaining, over-apologizing, and overextending are forms of verbal clutter. Boundaries bring clarity: No, I can't take that on right now. Yes, I'd love to see you—but let's choose a time that works for both of us. These simple, direct expressions cut through noise and preserve relationships by setting healthy expectations.

Relational minimalism also recognizes that not every interaction has to be filled. Silence has value. Sharing space without constant words can deepen comfort: a walk with a friend, a quiet meal, a moment of stillness. Connection isn't always talking; often it's simply being together.

When we strip away the clutter of performance, overcommitment, and noise, relationships become lighter and more real. We stop chasing approval and start sharing presence. We stop scattering ourselves across dozens of shallow ties and start investing deeply in the ones that matter. The art of less in relationships doesn't shrink love; it expands it. By removing distractions, we give room for sincerity, trust, and joy to grow.

WORK AND CREATIVITY:
DO LESS, DO BETTER

Work and creativity are two areas where the myth of "more" is especially loud. We are told that success requires longer hours, more projects, constant hustle. In creativity, the pressure is similar—more output, more content, more visibility. Yet just as clutter weakens a home and noise drowns a song, excess weakens our work. The art of less reminds us that doing fewer things with greater focus often produces deeper, richer results than scattering energy across endless tasks.

In work, this begins with prioritization. Many of us mistake busyness for productivity. We fill days with meetings, emails, and tasks that make us feel active but leave little of lasting value. The art of less at work distinguishes the essential from the trivial. Which projects align most closely with your values and strengths? Which tasks actually move the needle? What can be delegated, delayed, or discarded? This doesn't just lighten the workload; it sharpens the impact of what you choose to keep.

Boundaries play a role here, too. A career shaped by "more" quickly collapses into burnout. Saying no to unnecessary projects, limiting after-hours availability, and protecting rest are not signs of weakness; they are acts of sustainability. Work done from exhaustion is rarely excellent. Work done from balance often shines. The art of less permits a career defined not by sheer volume but by meaningful contribution.

Creativity thrives under similar principles. It's tempting to think that more tools, ideas, and output will make us better artists, writers, or makers. Often, creativity flourishes most when limits are embraced: a page a day that becomes a book, a limited palette that births a style, a single hour of uninterrupted focus that produces what a scattered day could not. Clearing distractions—buzzing phones, open tabs, constant multitasking—creates conditions for depth.

Vignette: A songwriter sits with one guitar and a legal pad. No plug-ins, no scrolling, no perfect mic. She hums the same line for twenty minutes until the melody clicks. The song arrives not because she had more, but because she gave her attention to less.

Perhaps most importantly, the art of less in work and creativity restores joy. When we no longer measure ourselves by volume, we rediscover the pleasure of immersion—of giving our best to a single task, of finding flow in a project that matters. Doing less but better is not laziness; it is mastery.

RHYTHM AND RITUAL:

A SUSTAINABLE CADENCE

One of the most overlooked benefits of living

with less is the way it creates rhythm. When we strip away excess, what remains is not emptiness but pattern—a cadence to life that feels steady, nourishing, and sustainable. This rhythm often expresses itself through ritual: small, repeated practices that ground us in what matters.

Morning, for instance, is often cluttered with urgency: checking messages, scanning headlines, rushing through routines. Yet with a few deliberate choices, morning can become ritual instead of chaos. Light a candle. Stretch in silence. Write a single line of gratitude. Brew coffee without multitasking. The ritual doesn't need to be long; its power is in its repetition.

Evenings can be designed to close the day with calm: a few pages of a book, a screened-off meal, a walk as the light fades. Weekly and monthly rhythms also steady us: family dinner on Sundays, a friend call every Friday, a solo day once a quarter to reset. These practices are not indulgent; they're structural beams that hold up the week.

Importantly, rituals in the art of less are not rigid rules. They're flexible, shaped by season and circumstance. If a morning ritual sometimes becomes a mid-afternoon pause, it is no less valuable. What matters is not strict adherence but the intention behind it. Rituals are there to serve us, not to burden us.

COMPOSITION OVER ACCUMULATION

At its core, the art of living with less is not about deprivation, but composition. It is the creative act of shaping a life that feels whole, balanced, and meaningful with fewer distractions. It is about asking: What belongs here? What does not? What makes the picture of my life clearer, richer, more beautiful?

When we apply this artistry to possessions, time, thoughts, relationships, and work, we discover a freedom that accumulation could never provide. Instead of being scattered by clutter, we are grounded by coherence. Instead of being overwhelmed by excess, we are uplifted by essentials. Life doesn't feel smaller when we choose less; it feels sharper, more vivid, more alive.

The beauty of this approach is its adaptability. There is no single formula for minimalism, no rigid rulebook that determines success. For one person, the art of less may mean a simplified home filled only with essentials. For another, it may mean a slower pace of work or a rhythm of daily rituals. For still another, it may mean clearing mental clutter and protecting time for creativity. Each life is its own canvas, each decision a brushstroke, each day a chance to refine the composition.

And like any art, it requires practice. Some days we overfill the canvas, saying yes to too much or letting possessions creep back in. Other days we strip away too much and feel deprived. Over time, the act of adjusting becomes part of the art. Minimalism is not a finished product; it is a living practice, evolving as we grow.

The reward is a life that feels both lighter and fuller. Lighter, because we no longer carry what we don't need. Fuller, because we have room to savor what we do. This is the paradox of less: by removing what distracts, we make space for what nourishes. By living with fewer things, we live with more joy. By simplifying, we uncover complexity's true companion—clarity.

And so, the art of less is not really about subtraction. It is about making room. Room for gratitude, for presence, for connection, for rest, for creativity, for joy. It is about creating a life spacious enough to hold what matters most.

As we move into the final chapter, the journey comes full circle. We began by naming the noise of a culture obsessed with more. We explored gratitude, comparison, community, and the corporate mirage. We looked at the relationships that either drain or sustain us. Now, with the art of less as our practice, we arrive at the question that started it all: How do we find sunshine every day?

The last chapter will not be about grand gestures or sweeping changes. It will be about the ordinary—the daily choices, small moments, and subtle shifts that allow us to experience joy not someday, but now. Because the sunshine we are searching for is not waiting on the horizon. It is already here, hidden in the ordinary light of today.

CHAPTER TWELVE
FINDING SUNSHINE EVERY DAY

Sunshine is not only a metaphor for joy or hope — it is a daily reminder that light is always available, even after the darkest night. The final step in our journey is learning to see and savor that light in ordinary moments. This isn't about chasing peak experiences or waiting for "someday" when conditions are perfect. It is about cultivating the ability to notice joy in the here and now.

Finding sunshine every day begins with attention. Too often, we move through life on autopilot, missing the details that could nourish us. We overlook the warmth of morning coffee, the laughter of a child, the colors of a sunset, the comfort of a familiar song. These moments slip past because our focus is elsewhere — on deadlines, worries, or the constant lure of "more." Sunshine is present, but unseen.

The practice is simple: slow down enough to notice. Pause, even briefly, and ask: What is good in this moment? Sometimes the answer will be small — a soft breeze, a smile from a stranger, a quiet corner of calm. Other times, it may be larger — a breakthrough at work, a deep conversation with a loved one, or an unexpected kindness. The size matters less than the recognition. Every act of noticing becomes an act of gratitude, and gratitude, as we've seen, multiplies joy.

TOUCHSTONES OF LIGHT

Another part of finding sunshine daily is creating touchstones of positivity. These are practices we weave into our routines that reliably lift the spirit.

For some, it may be journaling each morning. For others, a daily walk or a few minutes of meditation. Some find it in music, gardening, or simply stepping outside to feel the air. These touchstones are like open windows; they let light in on heavy days.

Picture this: the kettle clicks off. For once, you don't reach for your phone. You wrap your hands around the mug, inhale, and watch steam rise in the window's first light. Nothing has changed outside; something has softened inside. Sunshine doesn't always arrive with grandeur — sometimes it's in the quiet rituals we choose to notice. And the more we return to them, the more reliable they become. When storms come, we already know where the windows are.

To make this tangible, it helps to create a "sunshine toolkit" — a small set of practices you can reach for on any given day. Think of it as a handful of dependable rituals rather than a rigid checklist:

1. 3 × 3 Gratitude.

Name three specifics in thirty seconds, three times a day (wake, lunch, bedtime).

2. One-Window Walk.

Step outside once daily with no headphones, focusing on one sense — sight, sound, or scent.

3. Kindness Cue.

Tie one kind act to a daily trigger (after coffee send a thank-you text).

4. Five Breaths Reset.

Before a reply or decision, pause for five slow breaths.

5. Friction Finder.

Remove one tiny barrier to joy each week (coat by the door, book on the nightstand, shoes by the mat).

Individually, these are small. Collectively, they reshape how we experience the ordinary. Touchstones don't erase difficulty, but they keep light within reach.

THE SCIENCE OF SUNSHINE

Even the metaphor of sunshine has roots in our biology. Exposure to natural light helps regulate circadian rhythms, balances hormones, and stimulates serotonin — the brain's "mood stabilizer." That's why a walk outside can feel like a reset, why open blinds can lift spirits, why long stretches of gray weather can weigh us down. The body itself is wired to respond to light.

But it's not only sunlight in the literal sense. Psychologists note that attention itself acts like a light source for the mind. Where focus goes, energy follows. If we train attention to scan for what's good — a process gratitude helps with — we are literally reconditioning neural pathways to favor sufficiency over scarcity. In this sense, "finding sunshine" is not just poetic language; it's rewiring.

Try this: the next time you step outside, notice not only the sun but the shadows it creates. Both exist, but your gaze determines which takes center stage. The same is true of daily life.

SUNSHINE AND HARDSHIP

Importantly, sunshine is not about ignoring hardship. Life will always include stress, loss, and challenge. Pretending otherwise only leads to denial. But even in difficulty, there are beams of light — acts of kindness, lessons learned, resilience discovered. Finding sunshine is not about erasing pain, but about refusing to let pain be the whole story. It's about holding sorrow in one hand while still noticing beauty with the other.

Hardship reveals just how necessary this practice is. It is easy to notice sunshine when skies are clear. The challenge is holding onto it when life feels heavy — during seasons of grief, stress, or uncertainty. Yet these are the very moments when the practice becomes most powerful. Sunshine in hardship is not the absence of difficulty, but the presence of perspective.

The first step is reframing challenges. Instead of seeing difficulties only as obstacles, we can also view them as teachers. A season of waiting can cultivate patience. A season of loss can deepen compassion. A season of failure can sharpen resilience. This doesn't mean romanticizing hardship or pretending it is pleasant. It means acknowledging that alongside struggle, growth may also emerge.

Another practice is naming small victories. When life feels overwhelming, it's tempting to dismiss anything short of complete resolution. But even in dark times, small wins matter. Getting out of bed, showing up to work, making one honest phone call, preparing one simple meal — these are not trivial. They are evidence of resilience. Honoring them is a way of noticing light even when shadows press close.

Community is vital in hard seasons. When we are weighed down, our perspective narrows. Supportive relationships act as mirrors, reflecting hope back to us when we cannot see it ourselves. A friend's encouragement, a mentor's wisdom, or the quiet presence of someone willing to sit beside us — these are beams of light in otherwise dark rooms. Sunshine is often easier to borrow than to manufacture. Sometimes we need to lean on the light carried by others.

Gratitude, too, remains a lifeline. Even in sorrow, a single acknowledgment — I am thankful for breath today, for this meal, for one moment of laughter — keeps us tethered to light. Gratitude doesn't erase pain, but it prevents pain from being the only story. It trains the heart to keep looking, even when the view is dim.

And sometimes, finding sunshine means simply accepting the shadows. Light and dark coexist in every life. When we name the darkness honestly — this is hard, this hurts, this feels uncertain — we free ourselves to notice what else is present. Sunshine becomes more precious because it shines against contrast.

SEASONS OF SUNSHINE

The rhythm of sunshine is seasonal, both literally and metaphorically. In summer, light is abundant, easy to notice, almost taken for granted. In winter, it withdraws, and we feel its absence more acutely. Yet even in winter — both the meteorological and the metaphorical — light still exists. The crisp reflection off snow, the glow of candles, the warmth of companionship: sunshine adapts to the season, if we do too.

Think of the seasons of your own life. Youth often feels like summer — full of possibility, long days, and endless horizons. Midlife may resemble autumn, where light softens but deepens, illuminating harvests of meaning. Times of hardship echo winter, stark and stripped down, where even a flicker feels like a gift. Each season has its own kind of sunshine, and part of wisdom is learning to see it in its particular form.

A useful reflection: ask yourself, What kind of light does this season hold? The answer will change with time, but the practice of asking ensures you don't miss it.

HABITS THAT SUSTAIN JOY

Joy found once can feel like luck. Joy practiced daily becomes resilience. The key to sustaining sunshine is not intensity, but consistency — small, repeatable choices that weave positivity into the fabric of life until it becomes second nature.

Three principles matter most:

1. Simplicity.

Habits that are light enough to carry daily last longer than elaborate ones. A single line of gratitude is easier to sustain than a half-hour journaling session you dread. Ten minutes of walking is better than an hour-long workout you can't keep.

2. Integration.

Positivity lasts when woven into existing routines.

Gratitude with morning coffee, stretching while the kettle boils, silence before checking email. The less a practice feels like an "extra," the more naturally it sticks.

4. Flexibility.

Life shifts, energy rises and falls. A rigid practice shatters under pressure; a flexible one bends. If you miss gratitude at night, do it in the morning. If a walk is impossible, step outside for five deep breaths. Sunshine isn't perfection; it's returning.

Community also strengthens these habits. Just as negative relationships drain us, positive ones sustain us. Share your practices with a friend, partner, or group. A quick text — What's one good thing from today? — spreads light and keeps the rhythm alive. Joy multiplies when it is shared.

Reflection deepens sustainability. Every so often, pause to notice how life feels with these habits in place. Are you calmer, more grounded, more present? Recognizing progress reinforces the desire to continue. Without reflection, habits can feel like chores. With reflection, they become reminders of growth.

And perhaps most importantly: sustain joy by granting yourself permission to rest. Some days, you will forget. Some days, the practices will slip. That is not failure; that is humanity. The danger is not in missing a day but in giving up entirely. Sustainable sunshine means forgiving yourself quickly and beginning again. The sun rises every day — and so can you.

Over time, you'll know it's working not because life is flawless, but because you recover more quickly after frustrations, sleep a little easier, scroll a little less, and feel more present in ordinary moments. These are the subtle but unmistakable signs of a life brightened by habit.

SUNSHINE AT MINDSET

By now it's clear that sunshine isn't something we stumble upon only in rare, perfect moments. It's something we cultivate daily, through habits, perspective, and connection. What begins as deliberate effort — pausing to notice, naming gratitude, carving out silence — slowly becomes a way of seeing. Sunshine shifts from something external we chase to something internal we carry.

The most important realization is this: sunshine

is not a mood, it's a mindset. We cannot control every circumstance, but we can choose how we orient ourselves toward them. Some days will be heavy, and no amount of cheer will erase that. But even then, we can choose to keep looking for light, however small. Sunshine is not about denial; it's about balance.

This balance strengthens with practice. Gratitude keeps us grounded in sufficiency. Simplicity frees us from clutter. Boundaries protect peace. Healthy relationships and communities remind us we're not alone. Together, these create a foundation strong enough to hold both joy and sorrow, both abundance and loss.

Sharing sunshine is part of this transformation. Joy multiplies when given away. A kind word, a small gesture, an act of generosity — these brighten not only someone else's day but our own. The more we share, the more it returns.

Sunshine isn't meant to be a separate practice, reserved only for journals or rituals. It's meant to infuse the ordinary: sipping coffee slowly, listening fully, stepping outside for a breath, laughing freely. It's meant to remind us that enough is not a future goal but a present reality. A life lit by sunshine does not wait for perfection; it practices presence.

THE JOURNEY'S END — AND BEGINNING

The journey we've taken together has been about peeling back the layers of excess to rediscover what was always waiting beneath: the quiet, steady light of enough. We've named the forces that pull us away — comparison, consumerism, toxic relationships, corporate hunger — and we've practiced the antidotes: gratitude, simplicity, boundaries, community, and presence. And now, in this final step, we return to where it all began: the search for sunshine in the ordinary days of our lives.

What we discover is that sunshine is not rare. It isn't locked away in exotic places, extraordinary achievements, or distant futures. It is here — in the warmth of morning light through a window, in a conversation that feels real, in the satisfaction of completing something with care. The problem is not its absence, but our distraction. When we slow down, when we remove the noise, we see that sunshine was never gone.

To live this way is to choose differently in a

culture that shouts for more. It is to say: I don't need constant comparison to feel worthy. I don't need endless possessions to feel secure. I don't need toxic voices to define me. I don't need to chase the shimmer of the corporate mirage. I already have enough, and enough is abundant. This defiance is not small; it is revolutionary.

But it is also gentle. Finding sunshine does not require a dramatic lifestyle overhaul. It requires daily choices — small, quiet, deliberate. To notice. To appreciate. To release. To connect. These choices, repeated again and again, create a life that feels lighter and brighter, even when the world grows heavy.

The beauty of this practice is that it ripples outward. One person who chooses gratitude inspires another. One community that values sufficiency instead of rivalry begins to change the culture around it. Sunshine shared multiplies. What begins as an individual practice becomes a collective light.

And so, the invitation is simple: begin where you are. Don't wait for a perfect moment, or a quieter season, or a grand epiphany. Sunshine is not something to prepare for — it is something to notice now. Look around: what is one thing, in this moment, that brings light? Begin with that. Tomorrow, look again. The day after, look again. Over time, these small acts will add up to a life shaped not by scarcity, but by sufficiency; not by rivalry, but by connection; not by "more," but by enough.

The title of this book is not accidental. Searching for Sunshine is not about a destination. It is about a way of traveling through life — with eyes open to beauty, with hearts open to gratitude, and with hands open to release what doesn't serve us. Sunshine is not something we chase. It is something we learn to see.

May you see it. May you live it. And may you carry its light into every ordinary day.

EPILOGUE

THE HORIZON OF ENOUGH

The end of a book is never really an end. It is a pause, a moment to take a breath before walking back into life. What comes next is not a program to follow, nor a checklist to complete. It is an invitation — to notice what is already here, to choose what matters, and to return when you forget.

Finding sunshine has never been about waiting

for a perfect someday. It has always been about seeing what is present in the ordinary. The warm mug in your hands, the laughter of someone you love, the quiet space before the day begins — these are not background details, they are light. They are anchors to the truth that joy is available now.

The world will keep insisting on more: more possessions, more achievements, more comparisons. And it will always offer the same promise — that enough is just one step beyond where you are. You already know how hollow that pursuit feels. The invitation here is to live differently. To choose sufficiency in a culture that worships scarcity. To look at your life and say, this is enough, and enough is beautiful.

This doesn't mean pretending life is without struggle. Darkness is real: loss, disappointment, uncertainty. Sunshine is not about denying shadows; it's about remembering they are not the whole picture. Sometimes the light is large and radiant. Sometimes it is only a flicker. But even then, it matters. Especially then, it matters.

The practices in these pages — gratitude, simplicity, boundaries, community, presence — are not meant to be heavy burdens. They are touchstones. Use them when you need them. Adapt them as life shifts. And when you drift back toward clutter, rivalry, or hurry, don't scold yourself. Simply return. Return to noticing. Return to gratitude. Return to enough.

In the end, this is not about subtraction. It is about making room. Room for rest. Room for connection. Room for joy. The art of less has always been the art of more — more meaning, more clarity, more life in every moment.

Carrying the light forward means choosing, again and again, to resist the myth of scarcity. It means protecting your peace with boundaries, curating what you allow in your home and heart, and surrounding yourself with people who celebrate rather than compete. It means remembering that joy is multiplied in community, and that light, when shared, never diminishes.

The journey does not close here. It begins again each morning, in each small choice to notice, to slow down, to choose enough. That is the real revolution: not a single decision, but a pattern of returning.

Carrying the light does not mean living in constant brightness. It means trusting that even when life grows heavy, the sun has not disappeared. It means learning to look for the flickers — a kind word, a small victory, a moment of stillness — and letting them remind you that joy is not gone, only hidden. Sometimes, the light comes from within. Other times, we borrow it from the people who love us, the communities that hold us, the practices that steady us. Either way, the light remains.

You will not walk this path perfectly. None of us do. There will be weeks when clutter creeps back in, when comparison gets loud, when gratitude feels distant. That does not erase the journey. It only makes the next return more meaningful. The sun rises every morning. So can you.

In time, you may discover that these small daily choices ripple outward. One act of gratitude encourages another. One healthy boundary gives someone else courage to draw their own. One community that values presence over performance begins to shift the culture around it. The light you carry is not only for you. It is for the people who walk beside you, for the ones who will come after you, for a world that desperately needs reminders that enough is possible.

This is the gentle defiance we are called to: to say

no when the world insists on more, to say yes to the ordinary joy already within reach, to live with open hands and open eyes. It may not always feel radical, but it is. To choose sufficiency in a culture obsessed with accumulation is to resist. To find light in the ordinary is to rebel against despair.

As these pages close, the invitation is simple: begin where you are. Don't wait for the right season, the right mood, the right plan. Look up. Look around. What is one thing, right now, that brings you light? Start there. Tomorrow, start again. Slowly, these moments will weave into a rhythm, and that rhythm into a life that feels both lighter and fuller.

Sunshine is not something to chase. It is something to see, something to practice, something to share. It is not locked in the distance. It is here, in the ordinary, waiting for your attention.

Carry it forward. Carry it gently. Carry it persistently, imperfectly, but always with hope. And may you discover, again and again, that the light you seek is already here — within reach, within you, within every day.

This QR code connects you to a collection of my projects—original music, books, and products I've created. I invite you to explore and enjoy what I've been working on.

https://lynktu.com/Michael/Projects